THRIVING AMIDST CANCER Ⅱ : A GENERAL'S FOCUS ON HOPE WHILE FIGHTING BLADDER CANCER

Roger VanderKolk

Blauw Shack Media

Blauw Shack Media

ISBN: 979-8-9867313-4-6 (paperback)
ISBN: 979-8-9867313-5-3 (hardcover)

Cover Art by Kirstin Vincent

Dedicated to Brigadier General Bruce Wiley VanderKolk. Forever in our hearts. Forever a legacy for us to strive.

Foreword

Reflecting on the life of a friend, Bruce VanderKolk, a variety of key words come to mind. We worshiped, worked, and prayed together as we each sought to serve the Lord at South Side Christian Church in Springfield, Illinois.

Bruce was a kind, gentle guy who loved his wife and sons as well as our church family. His soft words were full of tenderness and compassion, but also carried the voice of one who meant business and no nonsense. His sense of humor quietly found its way into our conversations.

Mr. V. Was focused and organized. Upon retirement, Bruce began to help at the church, including attempting to organize financial records, job descriptions, and regular church practices resulting in a detailed and incredibly organized policy handbook.

When he softly asked you to do a job, somehow you just could not say, "No". Perhaps his work with the Illinois State Police gave him a voice of authority.

He was a natural for a chair of committees, served as an elder, and taught adult Bible class. He was prepared and spoke with authority. I have lost track of the number of committees where we worked together to further the church's impact. When faced with opinions that ran contrary to his ideas, Mr. V. Treated others with respect and genuinely listened to the other person to seek common ground. People listened and learned, because he cared to do his very best in every endeavor he tackled.

My heart beat with anticipation when introduced to the draft of the book "Thriving Amidst Cancer II: A General's Focus on Hope While Fighting Bladder Cancer". As I read the text, my emotions were mixed.

Passages relating to his family and events in their lives often brought smiles. However, his description of health issues, treatments, and moments of family love, caused tears to blur my vision. Blending his words with those of his son, equally talented with words, provided thoughtful moments of a family who cared for each other and for the Lord.

I expect I have never met a more caring, dedicated, gentle fellow who loved the Lord with all of his heart and energy. It was a joy to know and work with Bruce.

Kathryn Ransom

Cancer

I Respect No One

I respect no one.
Not the young nor the old.
Not the rich nor the poor.
Like a thief in the night,
I prey upon the unexpected.

I am silent,
> *For awhile.*
You do not hear me;
>> *You do not see me;*
>>> *You cannot sense me*
I am there but not seen.

You cannot run,
> *You cannot hide.*
You may be strong,
> *I am stronger.*
You may be on top,
> *I will bring you down.*
The sun may shine,
> *I will bring storms.*

1

I invade your structure;
        Invisible.
I take over space,
        Multiplying.
I destroy as I go,
        Killing good;
        Spreading death.

On my terms I will
        Reveal myself.

(Spoken by Cancer)

Oct 17, 2015
Bruce W. VanderKolk

Preface

Returning Readers

As the title implies, this book is the second in a series of books designed to provide messages of hope and encouragement to those facing medical or other struggles. Much of the first section of this book is copied from the previous book so that the new reader can gain knowledge and appreciation for Dad. If you have read the previous book, feel free to skip to the "Conclusion to Bruce's Story" section.

Author's Right to Write

My right to write came through the cancer journey with my mother, my grandmother, a cousin, and my father Bruce. I can relate to what your family is going through because my family has gone through a similar journey. After studying Bruce's journal, I can empathize with your experience and pull tidbits from the multitude of his experiences with major illnesses to provide advice on how to have hope during the struggle.

Perhaps my defining characteristic of a right to write about Bruce's journey is that he was my father.

I can tell you story after story after story of personal observations of how Bruce did not let his struggles with cancer and other illnesses negatively affect his daily life. One example: In June of 2013, my parents drove from their home in northern Illinois to my house in Woodbury, a suburb of St. Paul, MN. As you'll later read, this was during the time when Bruce was 4 years free from the prostate cancer but he was still dealing with the various side effects from the removal of the prostate.

Despite all of his issues, we had a great weekend. We took a day and drove to Duluth, MN, and explored the famed North Shore. We also visited Superior, WI, even making plans to come back and visit the Apostle Islands at a future time. Back in the Twin Cities, Dad and Mom made a couple of trips to downtown Stillwater, MN, which was one of their favorite places, especially the candy store. After I was finished working for the day, Dad and I went to the local shooting range. I even was able to convince them to attend a worship service at the church I was attending that was very contemporary (they preferred a traditional service). It was a great weekend because Dad focused on others rather than himself.

There are many other examples as well, such as the family trip we made to Disney in January of 2011; Easter in Minneapolis later in 2011; and many more.

Bruce was an expert on how to thrive during cancer, having battled one serious illness after another between the years of 2009 to 2017. Unfortunately he is no longer around to offer this advice to others engaged in similar struggles. That's why I'm sharing my exposition of his message with you.

Treatment of Bruce's Writings

In many respects this book was easy to write because the bulk of the text was pulled from various writings of Bruce's while he was fighting cancer and other diseases. At the time of his passing, he had gone through and made some grammar improvements, but it was necessary to make some revisions to his writings in order to have the work published. The grammar was improved in certain areas to improve the presentation of his words, but the content and message behind the writings is unchanged.

To foster anonymity, names of the specific physicians, medical facilities, and friends that Bruce recorded in his journal have been removed from this book. The word "doctor" is used to disguise the specific medical practitioner and the words "medical facility" are used to disguise the specific medical practice that Bruce recorded in his journal.

Sometimes, Bruce was very technical and detailed in his writings about the various conditions of the cancer or illness. For the most part, this information was included in the book because it might connect with people going through the same struggle and provide some level of comfort and/or encouragement.

All non-journal writings by Bruce during his struggle are referenced at the conclusion of the writing with his name and date of the writing.

The remainder of the book is written by the author. This includes the call-outs, the concept of thriving amidst the disease, and other content. The goal of this content is to peer into Bruce's life and project what he would want to convey.

Special treatment has been applied to the fonts of the two authors: Bruce's words will be treated in *Italics* format while the words of the author will be normal font.

The Second in a Series

When this project was started, the initial plan was to transform Dad's journal into one book. However, the amount of content that was in his journals quickly led to the realization that two books would be necessary to adequately deliver Dad's message. A third has since been added, making this series a trilogy.

The books are as follows:

- Book 1: Dad's initial entrance into the journey through serious diseases, primarily prostate cancer.
- Book 2: Having successfully beaten prostate cancer, Dad was looking forward to a period of good health. Instead, he found himself fighting bladder cancer from 2014-2017.
- Book 3: The trilogy wraps up with a chronicle of early 2018 until Dad's passing. The remainder of the book is a testament to the legacy he left behind.

Each of the books includes a section of key points from Dad's life that applies to those fighting serious illnesses. These are quick, simple guides for the reader to access when times get tough.

What This Book Is / Isn't

This book is a re-bundling of Dad's journals from the moment he learned that he likely had bladder cancer.

The last chapter in the book is meant to be interactive: twenty-one keys to thriving have been pulled from Dad's journals and compiled in this section. At the conclusion of each key is a blank space where you are encouraged to write notes for your current and future self. Please use this as a tool and refer back to it as often as necessary as you progress through the valley of the shadow of death.

The subtitle of the book is "A General's Focus on Hope While Fighting Bladder Cancer". Dad was fortunate to progress in his career in the military to the point where he was promoted to Brigadier General. This is significant for this book for two reasons. First, Dad was in rare company when he became general: there are only 231 generals in the U.S. Army at one time. By way of comparison, there are over 400 players in the NBA, over 1,000 players in Major League Baseball, and over 1,600 players in the NFL. This exclusivity provided Dad with credibility as he was able to achieve something that very few people attain.

Second, as a life-long military man, he created plans, back-up plans, and back-up plans for the back-up plans. He applied this to every facet of his life so it is not a big stretch to assume that he had plans to combat the illnesses he faced. But as you'll read, not only were those plans to combat the illness, the plans also focused on how Bruce would thrive during the struggle.

That being said, Dad would not view his battle plan as being inclusive of medical advice. This book does not offer any cures or treatments. This book is not intended to remedy your illness or symptoms.

Disclaimer

The author is not a doctor nor any type of medical professional. Bruce was not a doctor nor any type of medical professional. The following is a recording of one patient's walk through prostate cancer, thyroid issues, skin cancer occurrences, eye issues, bladder cancer, and other medical issues. Nothing in this book should in any way be construed as medical advice.

This book and all that it contains is for reference only and no medical advice is offered. Consult your medical professional.

Introduction

The Inspiration

On February 18th, 2018, Bruce Wiley VanderKolk passed from this earth to his heavenly reward. His passing was sudden, shocking, and unexpected but not altogether a surprise. Bruce had cheated death many times throughout his life starting immediately after college graduation when he was sent to Vietnam. Later there were battles with several different types of cancer as he got older. Sooner or later, we all knew that the odds were in cancer's favor and that it would likely ultimately prevail and claim Dad as yet another victim. We all realized that our time on this earth is limited and that ultimately we will exit. After watching him fight successfully against the cancers (plural intended), we thought that he had outwitted death and we would all have more time together.

But there was another factor in his family called heart attacks. His father had died of a heart attack in his early 70's. His father's father had died of a heart attack in his early 70's. As Dad neared that age, despite all the battles with cancer, he felt that he would break the cycle and live past his early 70's. Life is cruel however. Dad didn't make it into his mid-70's. At the time of his passing, he was coming up to his 73rd birthday.

Deep down, Dad must have realized that his time on earth was limited. He began chronicling his battles with cancer for two reasons. First, he used the time spent writing in introspection about his battle trying to make sense of the suffering and illnesses. The second, and more important aspect of the writing, was to be a beacon for others that are (or will be) going through similar situations.

When Dad received the initial call from his doctor in 2009 about elevated PSA levels, he began chronicling his situation in a writing he called "A Series of Events". This book uses that story as a foundation and adds other writings of Dad's. These are interspersed with further advice that we are sure he would have written had he not passed so soon.

Dad would have wanted his trials to help inspire others to not just merely survive when they are going through cancer or some other type of life-threatening disease but to actually thrive and to be a beacon to others. While the book specifically deals with Dad's experience with bladder cancer, the principles that he wrote about apply to other critical diseases as well.

Thank you for taking this journey with us. It is our hope and prayer that this book is a gift of encouragement to you or someone you know going through a difficult situation. It is also our hope and prayer that you become a beacon of hope to those around you.

Bruce

The eldest of two sons, I was privileged to not only grow up in his household, but also to enjoy a close relationship with him until the day he left this earth.

Sure, there were the normal squabbles during adolescence, but in my mind these were few and far between because I saw myself as a problem-free child (I am sure that other family members would disagree with this statement, which they are free to do in their own book). It also probably helped in our relationship that Dad was often out of the house, either traveling for his day job or his weekend job with the Illinois National Guard. His work with the church also took him away from the house a couple of times a month for evening meetings. If we are being completely honest, there was a healthy bit of fear in our relationship as well. Nothing straightened up a teenager like the words, "wait until your father gets home".

When I moved away to attend university in Indiana, our relationship grew stronger. The distance and not being under the same roof at the same time likely were key contributors, but I also think our relationship got stronger because Dad saw me coming into my own. I was fortunate to attend a Christian university and was blessed to form a friendship with a group of spiritually strong young men. Corrections were few and far between when I was at college: Dad didn't have to worry about me partying, skipping class, carousing, drinking, etc. The strongest disagreement we had was when I was stubborn about not seeking surgery for a torn ACL because I thought it would heal on its own. After several "discussions", including a classic metaphor about an old farmer who drowned because he refused to recognize God's provision during a flood, I had the surgery. Of course Dad was right. Today, over 25 years later, the repaired knee continues to function perfectly.

I am sure that Dad had some disappointment that I didn't branch off in his career direction, but like many sons, I was determined to make my own way. Today, as I approach the age that Dad was when he took early retirement, I long to go back and follow his career path because I am still likely decades away from retirement.

Through 45 years of being his son, Dad was calm, methodical, slow to anger, eager to work with me to tackle life successfully, and many, many more adorning adjectives. My hope is that this book provides a glimpse into the man that Dad/Bruce was and that it is a blessing to your life.

But Also Dad

The reader will notice that Dad is referred to as "Bruce" throughout the beginning of this book. This is intentional. The focus of the book is sharing about how Bruce was able to live an example to others while he was fighting multiple illnesses and diseases.

If you read book 1, you will already be familiar with Bruce, enough so that this book will quickly transition to "Dad". This is also intentional. Once "Bruce" is established, it is necessary to bring his relationship with his family back into focus because it was an important aspect of his example of thriving.

PART ONE
WHO WAS BRUCE VANDERKOLK?

Bruce's Life Synopsis

Michigan: The Early Years

Bruce was born on March 16th, 1945 to Wiley and Violet VanderKolk. He was the youngest of two sons. With six years between the brothers, Bruce was literally the baby of the family. The VanderKolks lived on a farm in southwest Michigan with arable farming land, but the primary focus was dairy farming. Life on a dairy farm was notoriously hard; there were no vacation days or sick days because the cows required milking twice a day, everyday. It is reasonable to believe that this lifestyle created an intense work ethic with Bruce as he grew up.

The farm was located in a remote area; the nearest large city was Grand Rapids, about an hour's drive away. Bruce spent his entire educational experience in Hopkins, a small town. As he struggled through the education system, Bruce aspired to go away to college, a dream that was supported by his parents. In the end he selected Michigan State University in East Lansing, MI. To him it was far enough away from home to build his independence, but near enough to go back for holiday visits.

MSU to Vietnam

Life at Michigan State University was everything Bruce hoped for: Parties, parties, and more parties. And perhaps a bit of studying. Actually, a lot more than a bit because Bruce was able to graduate with a degree in Chemistry with honors.

It was during this time that Bruce decided to focus; first on finding a life partner. He chose wisely and renewed an earlier relationship with Donna Townsend, his eventual wife of 49 years.

The second area of focus was the developing conflict in Vietnam, specifically the consideration in the government of instituting a draft for young males, one of which was Bruce. There was the risk that he would be subject to the draft. Bruce applied his analytical mind to the options: Option 1 was to proceed ahead into the workforce and hope (and pray) that his number didn't come up in the draft. If his number did come up, then he would have to report to Basic Training and more than likely be in the Infantry.

Option 2 was to be proactive and sign up for the Reserve Officers' Training Corps (ROTC) at Michigan State. This would guarantee that he would serve in the military and all but guarantee service in Vietnam, but it would give him the ability to determine his path, likely away from the infantry.

Bruce chose option 2 and joined the ROTC program. Once he graduated from ROTC, it was time to report to Vietnam. He and Donna had recently married. However their time together was short lived; Bruce was going to Vietnam as an Artillery officer.

Bruce didn't speak much about his time in Vietnam, as is common with most veterans. Later in life he did do some writing about his time there, which will be the subject of future publishing works.

Post Vietnam

It isn't exactly clear when Bruce developed the habit of being proactive, but it was demonstrated in Vietnam. He started his job search before he returned to the States from his tour of duty. Similar to drafting a sleeper player that ends up being a Hall of Famer, the Illinois State Police (ISP) took a chance on the young man who applied for a chemistry position in the Forensic Science division. It probably didn't hurt his chances that he did an internship with the ISP while he was in college.

This professional relationship lasted for several decades. Bruce was instrumental in the transformation of the ISP Forensic Division from an after-thought to one of the leading departments in the entire country. He eventually retired from the ISP at a rank of Commander of the Forensic Science Division.

Bruce was obligated to continue his relationship with the US Armed Forces in the near term after his return from Vietnam. He transferred to the Army Reserves but was unable to find a spot in the contingent based in Springfield, IL. He thus transferred to the Illinois National Guard which had a spot for an officer at his level at the local base, Camp Lincoln. He rose in the ranks until he retired as a Brigadier General.

After his retirement from the Illinois State Police, Bruce was actually not ready for retirement. He lent his incredible experience of improving forensic laboratory systems to a couple of consultant projects. He even briefly considered going to Iraq to do the same, but was dissuaded by the family; Iraq in the early 2000's was not a particularly safe environment. Instead he went to work at his church in various capacities to lend his expertise in leadership and organization to improving the day-to-day operation of his church in Springfield, IL.

Cancer: Bruce's Unwanted Stalker

Bruce served faithfully in the United States Army in Vietnam, with no complaint. When the airplanes started applying chemical defoliant to the jungle surrounding the bases where he was located, there were no complaints. It was only later, much later, when he and the rest of the world came to learn the human cost of that defoliant, also known as Agent Orange, on Bruce and the thousands of other soldiers serving in Vietnam.

Cancer started to make its presence felt with Bruce in the most innocuous of circumstances: skin issues, first the ears, then the nose. Consequently, Bruce began spending quite a bit of time with a medical team in Illinois. Later in life, when he was transitioning to life in Florida, it would continue to come back, but this time required a complete face scrubbing to reduce the problem areas. The same type of face scrub that makes exposure to sun extremely painful (while he was in Florida, where it is not possible to walk outside without being exposed to direct sunlight. The pain must have been tremendous). But, as before, he did the treatment without any complaints.

After leaving the workforce, Bruce engaged in that age old practice of retirees everywhere: constant doctor visits to make sure that his health was on track. He was always a lover of good food (particularly a good hamburger) and as a result struggled with weight, cholesterol, and pre-diabetes symptoms.

The previous book described Bruce's journey through prostate cancer and thyroid issues. Cancer again takes center stage in this book as well, except this time the cancer is attacking the bladder.

Faith Journey

Faith's Importance to Bruce

Bruce's faith in God was the cornerstone of his life. Bruce's faith was not a static, go to church once a month, type of faith. No, his was an active faith. He believed that one of the purposes for his being on this earth was to bring more people to faith in God so that they could enjoy the benefits of everlasting life in heaven.

Faith is what drove Bruce to thrive in the face of many devastating illnesses. He clung to God's promises during dark days and he knew that how he lived his life would be an example to others. He was not afraid to let others know of his faith. Bruce wrote the following synopsis of his faith journey in 2008, before his struggle with prostate cancer started.

Bruce VanderKolk Personal Testimony (Bruce)

I grew up in the Reformed Church of America. I cannot remember a time when my parents did not faithfully go to church and take their children. I was baptized as an infant and as I grew older participated in Sunday School, Wednesday evening catechism, and Sunday night activities. When I approached High School, I joined the church and to do so I appeared before the elders to answer questions about my faith, my commitment, and biblical knowledge.

After High School I attended college and upon graduation I entered the US Army. It was during college and my initial time in the service that I became less active and committed to attending church. However, when I was sent to Vietnam I realized that I could not mentally survive unless I started again to turn my life over to God's care and providence. This time in my life was a gradual re-awaking and it has continued to this day. I do not consider "the race" to be over and realize that there is much more to learn and to do in service for God. Where this will lead I do not know, however, I try to be vigilant about not closing any doors.

After military service, my wife and I attended the Presbyterian Church, the Orthodox Presbyterian Church and for the last 30 years South Side Christian

Church in Springfield, IL. With each passing year I have steadily grown in my spiritual life. In June of 1978 I was baptized by immersion. After studying the scriptures I could not see where baptism is proclaimed in the Bible except by immersion.

I have served as a deacon and several years as an elder at South Side Christian Church. I have taught several years of Adult Bible School and have assisted in several other ministries of the church. After retiring from the Illinois State Police in 2001, I went to work at South Side Christian Church as the Church Administrator. I later moved into the Equipping and Assimilating ministry on a part time basis. In April 2010, after the Senior Minister left, I served as the Executive Minister overseeing the staff and ministers. I have participated in providing training to other elders or potential elders on the practical aspects of being an elder and other leadership issues. This has been done at South Side Christian Church, Restoration House Ministries in New Hampshire, and at Maritime Christian College in Prince Edward Island.

I have gone through many personal challenges in addition to my Vietnam experience. I have gone through Donna's cancer over 20 years ago, a stroke by our youngest son while he was in High School, personal injuries and cancer resulting in 10 major surgeries. I have experienced the "highs and lows" that come with these. I have several times asked God why? Through all of this my faith has grown but I am not where I should be. God has been good and I have been blessed. I believe the following two statements:

"God is good all the time. All the time God is good."

"The storms of our life prove the strength of our Anchor."

Bruce W. VanderKolk (April 21, 2008, revised September 23, 2015)

Bruce's Faith in God and His Service (written by Bruce VanderKolk)

1. *Grew up going to the Reformed Church in Bradley, MI*
   a. *Was sprinkled when he was in Junior High and had catechism classes at that time*
2. *Attended 1st Presbyterian Church in Joliet, IL 1969*
   a. *Part of a small group, and had a retreat at Stronghold, Oregon, IL*
3. *Presbyterian Church in Geneseo, IL 1970-1973*

4. *Orthodox Presbyterian Church in Wheaton, IL 1973-1977*
    a. *Headed up the nursery*
5. *South Side Christian Church, Springfield, IL 1978-2011*
    a. *Immersed June of 1978*
    b. *Sponsor of Bible Bowl*
    c. *Deacon*
    d. *Elder*
    e. *Chairman of Elders*
    f. *Bible School Teacher*
        i.   *U&I Class – College age Students*
        ii. *Adult Bible School classes*
    g. *Church Administrator – Paid Position – 2001-2006*
    h. *Assimilation and Equip Coordinator*
    i. *Executive Minister 2010*
    j. *Volunteered at homeless shelter*
6. *Attended Church of God, Oregon, IL*
    a. *Volunteered at homeless shelter*
7. *Anchor Christian Church, Bonita Springs, FL 2013-2018*
    a. *Elder*
    b. *Chairman of Missions Committee*
    c. *On building committee*
    d. *Chairman of 55+ ministry*
    e. *Adult Bible School teacher*

PART TWO
HOW THEN TO THRIVE?

Faith: The Foundation to the Path Forward

As you will read throughout the remainder of this book, Bruce relied on his faith as he faced one serious illness after another. Bruce spent countless hours throughout his life reading and studying the Bible. He came to the conclusion that for those that have faith in Him, God will not fail His children.

Following are two essays that Bruce wrote regarding his faith. The first was written during his battle with bladder cancer, but the message applies to his earlier diseases as well. The second is a reflection of the impact that his time in Vietnam played on his faith.

These two essays speak to the importance of faith for Bruce while he faced very different life-threatening situations.

_____

"He will not fail us"

<u>Psalm 91 (NIV)</u>
> 1 Whoever dwells in the shelter of the Most High
>   will rest in the shadow of the Almighty.
> 2 I will say of the Lord, "He is my refuge and my fortress,
>   my God, in whom I trust."
> 3 Surely he will save you
>   from the fowler's snare
>   and from the deadly pestilence.
> 4 He will cover you with his feathers,
>   and under his wings you will find refuge;
>   his faithfulness will be your shield and rampart.
> 5 You will not fear the terror of night,
>   nor the arrow that flies by day,
> 6 nor the pestilence that stalks in the darkness,

nor the plague that destroys at midday.

7 A thousand may fall at your side,
ten thousand at your right hand,
but it will not come near you.

8 You will only observe with your eyes
and see the punishment of the wicked.

9 If you say, "The Lord is my refuge,"
and you make the Most High your dwelling,

10 no harm will overtake you,
no disaster will come near your tent.

11 For he will command his angels concerning you
to guard you in all your ways;

12 they will lift you up in their hands,
so that you will not strike your foot against a stone.

13 You will tread on the lion and the cobra;
you will trample the great lion and the serpent.

14 "Because he loves me," says the Lord, "I will rescue him;
I will protect him, for he acknowledges my name.

15 He will call on me, and I will answer him;
I will be with him in trouble,
I will deliver him and honor him.

16 With long life I will satisfy him
and show him my salvation."

(Bruce) I am always amazed when those who have cancer outwardly appear to have a tranquil nature. I wish I could copy that DNA of tranquility into my own mind and personality. Maybe they are at peace with their situation and the outward appearance is real and not a brave front. Unfortunately, my situation has been displayed as that of a chameleon. To others I change my color to reflect an appearance of strength and acceptance. I try not to take the cancer seriously in front of others and when asked I reply, "I'm doing ok". I live a life externally of pretending that nothing really is wrong and a philosophy of "this too will pass- no big deal".

But it is a big deal; I just do not want to admit it outwardly. Besides, I have found that many people who have not experienced the trials of cancer do not want to talk about it, do not understand the emotions a person goes through, may even avoid you as if you have leprosy. My situation may even remind them of their own personal experience of cancer or of someone who had cancer and they do not want to bring to surface from the depths of inner parts of their mind the pain that they have gone through. This is where my other chameleon color comes in.

When alone my mind is in turmoil; it is constantly making my daily life one of contrasts, like a yo-yo that is ever moving up and down. One moment I may be up and the next I may be at the bottom of the yo-yo's cycle; a cycle that is in perpetual motion denying the laws of physics. I am in a 24/7 mode of operation as there appears no escape from the reality of cancer. It is there with you when you wake up, it is there with you in the morning hours, it is there with you when you go to the store, it is there with you when you may be entertaining, it is there with you when you're watching television at night, it is there with you when you go to bed and you pray to God for healing, it is there when for some reason you wake up during the night; it is always present, never ending. How do you explain that to someone who has not walked in the same shoes and does not have a grasp of the terrible experiences that cancer brings? In some ways, I think the mental aspects of dealing with cancer may be as bad or worse then the physical aspects of dealing with cancer.

I wish I had a magic formula to give you as you go through many trials, but I do not. Well intended people may say "just rely upon God", "out of adversity there comes good", "I know you will be ok", or "there are a lot of new treatments today that will help you". Well, thanks but this does not help. Sure, I appreciate their sincerity and attempts at giving hope, but words alone do not provide peace of mind; words do not heal.

I may sound cynical and maybe I am to some extent. However, as I have tried to come to grips with my cancer, I know I could not continue without drawing upon the strength given to us through our belief in God and the many comforting verses found in His Word. Does it totally solve my daily mental gyrations; no, but I cannot imagine what it would be like without His love and care for me to minimize those gyrations. I wonder how do those with cancer who do not have a relationship with God ever make it through the day? Where is their hope? The answer is they have no hope! You see I believe God truly understands my situation. And I fully understand that my way may not be His way.

There are many great Bible verses that give comfort and strength. Some of my favorites are found in the book of Philippians, such as:

"Rejoice in the Lord always. I will say it again: Rejoice! Let your gentleness be evident to all. The Lord is near. Do not be anxious about anything, but in everything, by prayer and petition, with thanks-giving, present your requests to

God. And the peace of God, which transcends all understanding, will guard your hearts and your minds in Christ Jesus. Finally, brothers, whatever is true, whatever is noble, whatever is right, whatever is pure, whatever is lovely, whatever is admirable-if anything is excellent or praiseworthy-think about such things. Whatever you have learned or received or heard from me, or seen in me-put it into practice. And the God of peace will be with you." Philippians 4:4-9 (NIV).

And:

"Forgetting what is behind and straining toward what is ahead, I press on toward the goal to win the prize for which God has called me heavenward in Christ Jesus." Philippians 3:13b-14 (NIV).

Finally, I return to the scripture quoted at the beginning of this writing, Psalm 91 (NIV): A Psalm of hope and comfort. How can we not find solace when we read the following about God?

- we will rest in the shadow of the Almighty
- He is my refuge and my fortress, … in whom I trust
- He will save you
- He will cover you with his feathers
- under His wings you will find refuge
- His faithfulness will be your shield and rampart
- He will command his angels concerning you to guard you in all your ways
- He will protect you, when we acknowledge His name.
- He will be with you in trouble
- He will deliver you and honor you

Do I expect my life to be a "bed of roses" because I put my trust in His words of hope and comfort? No. Do I expect that this life will pass away and there will be a more glorious life for eternity with our Lord and Savior? Yes.

May you seek comfort in knowing that what is coming is far greater than what you are going through now.

Bruce W. VanderKolk (5 November 2017)

How I Saw God's Faithfulness Through a War Situation

When I was asked to apply how the question of "how God is faithful?" to my experiences in Vietnam, I thought it was quite easy. In fact, I said it could be summed up in three words-"I came back". However, upon further reflection, I am not sure that this is an appropriate answer. I'm not sure because it could be implied that those who did not come back were unfaithful. I'm not sure it is an appropriate answer because God does not say that we will not encounter difficulties or even death. The more I pondered the question, the more difficult it was to find an answer.

Actually, the question of how we see God's faithfulness has nothing to do with a war situation. It could just as easily be applied to our work, a vacation, a sporting event or even here at the church. It does not matter what your setting, God is faithful to those who are faithful to him. He is faithful according to His plan, not ours. His faithfulness is shown by the fulfillment of His promises.

When I went to Vietnam, I had to realize I was not in control but that I had to put my trust in God. Once that happened, I was at peace. No longer did I fear the potential terrible consequences of war or death. And why? Because we are protected by the power of God and he will provide a spiritual deliverance according to his plan, not necessarily a physical deliverance.

If I was to modify the question, I would ask "How did I experience God's promises as a result of His faithfulness to me in a war situation". I experienced His promises in several ways. The most prominent were:

- An inner peace
- Strength to face another day
- Confidence
- Comfort
- Boldness
- Assurance
- Courage
- Encouragement
- Answered prayer

One way God comforts me I believe is by sending the words to songs into my mind and then the constant rhythmical repetition of the verses. One of these is the song "He Lives" by Gloria and Bill Gaither. The lyrics of the third verse of that song explains the peace of mind I felt. The verse speaks to the glory that we will *experience when we leave this life and enter heaven because of the gift delivered as a result of Jesus overcoming death. Because of Jesus and his sacrifice, we will one day live forever and ever with God.*

Is God faithful in a war situation? Yes

But the more important question is "Is God faithful at all times?"

The answer is Yes.

Bruce W. VanderKolk

Sometime between 2001 and 2005

Thriving

Life is Hard (Roger)

One of the most over-used phrases is that "Life is Hard". It generally is followed by a second phrase such as "get up" or "suck it up" that is meant to encourage the listener to overcome the hardness of life.

The reality is that yes, Life is Hard. Period. End of Story. A bit of faith coming in, but if you are a believer, the Bible makes it plain as day that life isn't a bed of roses. Sin has entered our world and we will never experience a life that is truly easy. Sure, we will all experience times of peace, but during those times, the universe is in the background planning, plotting, and scheming on how to bring pain, loss, or something equally as devastating back into our lives.

Psychology tells us that there are five stages of grief: Denial, Anger, Bargaining, Depression, and Acceptance. When we are faced with life-changing, devastating news, we will all go through these stages, ending at acceptance.

But after we have accepted the new reality, we must still determine how we will move forward with life. Faced with a life-threatening situation or illness, three options are open to us as we move forward:

1. We can surrender. We can give up and let the disease win. We can withdraw from society, friends, family and wait for the disease to achieve its ultimate goal of defeating the body.
2. We can survive. We can only do what is necessary to come out of the other side of the disease. We can throw all of the strength and resources that we can pull together to beat the disease.
3. We can thrive. Building upon the choice to survive, we can fight the disease. We can also work to ensure that our lives enrich those around us, whether it be family, friends, acquaintances, or society as a whole.

In the face of a life-threatening situation or illness, we will face the option of choosing one of these three options. The bad news is that life isn't fair: once we make a decision to choose one option such as to Thrive, life will continue to tempt us to change our minds. Even those who decide to Thrive will face the option of surrendering.

Despite all of the hardness that life threw at him, Dad made the decision to Thrive.

What it Means to Thrive

Whenever we are faced with a difficult situation, the immediate focus is just to survive the episode so that we can live to fight another day. There is absolutely nothing wrong with pursuing the survival path because it is valid: As finite creatures, we need to make sure that we do everything in our power to extend our life on this earth.

The problem comes when the survival path is the only path we choose. When the focus is solely on survival, after we are successful there is no further action moving forward. This is limiting, not only for the person going through the battle, but for society as a whole.

Webster defines the word "thrive" as: "to grow or develop successfully; to flourish or succeed; to progress toward or realize a goal despite or because of circumstances."

As he fought through his battles with cancer and other diseases, Dad came to realize that there are two types of thriving:

1. Thriving Internally - The first stage of thriving is learning how to flourish in spite of difficult circumstances. How to wake up in the morning and get out of bed. How to get the head and emotions in a good spot.
2. Thriving Externally - The second stage is taking the internal flourishing and packaging it as a tool to help others. Thriving is the act of blessing the lives of others. It is focusing not on yourself and your difficult situation, but focusing on how to improve the lives of others.

As you begin reading through what is essentially Dad's journals, you will see his path transform from one of survival to one that promoted both internal and external thriving. Whether he consciously realized it or not, Dad's path became a source of blessing for others, helping those around him going through battles to flourish despite or because of circumstances.

It is my goal to share his journey with the masses to increase the blessing of his journey through multiple struggles.

PART THREE
CONCLUSION TO BRUCE'S JOURNEY

2014

Introduction (Roger)

Returning readers will notice that Dad's story in this book is divided into time periods rather than by a particular phase of the fight against cancer. The reason for this is that his battle with bladder cancer wasn't confined to a specific time period. The diagnosis period was short and the treatment period was extremely long as the doctors attempted to control the disease. The time frame after the final surgery was also short.

The previous book concluded with Dad's journal entry in May, 2014. This section starts in October, 2014 when Dad began experiencing issues with his bladder.

October 9, 2014 (Bruce)

"It was the best of times, it was the worst of times." *That describes the phone call I received today from the doctor. You see, I called the medical facility about 10 days earlier because I was having brown flakes and blood in my urine. I had been experiencing the brown flakes for a few months but now I also had red "strings" which appeared to be blood around an object. The doctor scheduled me for a CT scan to make sure I was not having problems from a kidney stone (in June 2014, I spent a few days at a hospital in Florida with what was finally concluded as a kidney stone problem).*

The doctor personally called to explain that the good news was there were no masses, or kidney stones or any other issue manifested by the CT scan. The bad news was that because of my symptoms and the inability for the CT scan to show much of the bladder, the doctor had scheduled me for a cystoscopy which involves looking at the bladder with a scope (sounds terrible, but the doctor said it is not that bad-however, the doctor is doing the test and not receiving the test!)

I do not know what the future holds. It could simply be a result of too much strenuous exercise as I have been biking a lot of miles over the past few years and I have noticed that it sometimes has created discomfort when urinating. However, if it is cancer, then the future does not look that bright even if the cancer is cured; this is because of residual problems and "quality of life" issues. From my reading about bladder cancer it will make my prostate cancer procedure look like a piece of cake. Bladder cancer is the 6th highest rate of cancer.

As I have said before, when does it end? How many more problems must I face. How will I deal with this issue if it is cancer? Will I have a meltdown or face it with confidence and hope? Only time will tell. As you read further and I update this document you may find the answer.

Trust: The Key (Roger)

"I do not know what the future holds".

Dad likely wrote these words from a point of despondency. After navigating through countless medical issues over the past few years, he again was faced with news that he potentially was facing another serious disease. It must have been devastating to find himself thrust back into a fight against cancer.

But these words are powerful because they speak to a universal truth in this life: No one knows what tomorrow will hold. We close our eyes every night not knowing what we will experience when we awake the next day. If we are being honest, we really don't even know with confidence whether we will wake up the next day.

If you're a believer, then you at least have confidence that whatever troubles we have in this world, they pale in comparison to the glory we will have in the next world. We place our trust in the many words of encouragement and messages of Hope written in the Bible.

Consider these statistics from the Bible: The word "trust" is found 170 times in the New International Version of the Bible. The word "hope" is found 180 times in the New International Version of the Bible. If you were to start on the "trust" passages and then move to the "hope" passages, by reading only one verse a day, that would take nearly an entire year to read these messages of encouragement.

As believers, although we do not know for certain what tomorrow brings, we have hope in the eternal "tomorrow" because we trust in God.

The following passage brought hope to Dad's situation and will bring hope to your situation as well:

Romans 15:13 (NIV)

"May the God of hope fill you with all joy and peace as you trust in him, so that you may overflow with hope by the power of the Holy Spirit."

We don't know what tomorrow will bring. All we can do is put our trust in the One who has gone on record as saying that He will fill us with joy and peace so that we may **overflow** with hope. Other versions use the word "abound" or the phrase "bubbling over" in place of the word "overflow". We just don't have a little bit of hope. We have all the hope we need.

This is how we get up in the morning and make the choice to live a life that is a blessing to others despite the circumstances in our lives.

We have hope. Hope that is a result of our trust in God is the foundation of how we are able to thrive.

Oct 13, 2014 (Bruce)

Last week I had my six month ultrasound scan of my thyroid. Today I talked to the medical facility and was informed that the scan showed more nodules. As a result, the doctor wants to see me on Oct 22, 2014, about the results of the scan. This does not sound good as 1) the doctor wants to meet with me, and, 2) it has not been growing for a few years. I do not know what it means because it can mean 1) possibly cancer causing, and/or 2) the nodules can restrict the throat if there are too many or they become large.

Also I visited another medical facility too and got my stitches removed from an area on my right arm a couple of weeks ago. While there I received a copy of the report. The diagnosis read "Lichen Planus-Like Keratosis". I looked it up and it is an autoimmune problem. Not contagious but also no cure; can be treated if necessary. They do not know what causes it.

October 22, 2014

Met with the doctor today at the medical facility where the doctor wanted to meet with me about an ultrasound I had on my thyroid on October 8, 2014. The ultrasound was a follow-up 6 month checkup. The doctor wanted to meet as there were at least 3 and possibly 4 new nodules growing on my thyroid since the last scan in April, 2014. The doctor was concerned about this new growth and felt another biopsy should be done. The doctor also reiterated that at some point in time in the future I would need to have the thyroid removed. The doctor also said that it would be okay if I decided to do it now. After discussing it with Donna we decided to do the ultrasound. This is scheduled for October 30, 2014.

October 24, 2014

Well, is this the beginning of the end? I have been having some issues with brown and sometimes bright red flakes appearing in my urine. Associated with this at times was pain at the completion of urinating. I finally decided to have it checked out and called the doctor about the problem. The doctor scheduled me for a CT at a local medical facility

After about 4 days the doctor called personally and said the CT did not show any growths except for a couple of cysts on the kidneys. The doctor said this was not unusual. However, because of the problem I was having, the doctor wanted me to have a Cystoscopy (bladder scope). This was scheduled for October 24, 2014. This is not the most pleasant test (you can guess how it is performed). Anyway, I was able to watch on the screen as the procedure is a video of the inside of the bladder. In the bladder I had red areas and at least one larger dark red area. Based on this the doctor said I need to have a biopsy of these areas to see if they are cancer.

The biopsy will be done at a local medical facility as I need to be put out. The doctor said if it is cancer it may be a Transitional Cell Carcinoma which is limited to the inner lining of the bladder and has not gone into the muscle or further. It also could be a cystitis which is an inflammation of the bladder lining. The doctor said a cystitis is highly treatable and not to worry over the weekend (easy for the doctor to say). However, I have suspected something is not right and am concerned. I did not know how to read the doctor but I suspect the suspicion is that it is cancer. I must admit the video of those areas did not look good to me.

So, am I cancer free, or do I have thyroid cancer, or do I have bladder cancer, or do I have both? Thyroid cancer will result in surgery followed by treatments and a full body scan. Bladder cancer may or may not result in surgery-depends on what they find out during the biopsy. If it is cancer, the treatment will vary depending on the staging but in all cases probably will result in some type of chemo.

As I said above, is this the beginning of the end? I have been free of prostate cancer for almost five years. How many more bullets can I dodge?

Hope (Roger)

As stated previously, the word "hope" is found 180 times in the Bible. To some, that might seem like an excessive amount in a book that is a collection of 66 smaller books. The breakdown is roughly 50/50 between the Old and the New Testaments, but there are fewer mentions in the Old Testament.

Why does the Bible speak so much about hope? Because our world is dreadful, full of disease, violence, starvation, war, cheating, hunger, death, conflict, sickness, fear, drought, and countless other words that have been invented throughout history to describe how evil has penetrated our world.

It is no coincidence that the word hope is used so many times in the Bible. We truly need hope. Dad certainly needed to focus on his hope for a better tomorrow, his hope for a forever future in heaven. Despite surviving all of the diseases that tried to kill him in the previous book, he now faced the prospect of a double whammy: thyroid cancer and bladder cancer.

"How many more bullets can I dodge?"

This is how Dad closes the previous journal entry after learning that there is a high degree of probability that his latest foe will be bladder cancer. His hope in God gave Dad the strength to get up in the morning and fight these serious, potentially life-threatening diseases because they were only temporary.

Dad needed all 180 of those hope-related verses. Here are some particularly strong ones for those going through struggles in this life:

- Psalm 33:20: "We wait in **hope** for the Lord; he is our help and our shield" (NIV)

- Psalm 33:22: "May your unfailing love be with us, Lord, even as we put our **hope** in you." (NIV)
- Psalm 62:5-6: "Yes, my soul, find rest in God; my **hope** comes from him. Truly he is my rock and my salvation. He is my fortress, I will not be shaken." (NIV)
- Isaiah 40:31: "But those who **hope** in the Lord will renew their strength. They will soar on wings like eagles; they will run and not grow weary, they will walk and not be faint." (NIV)
- Micah 7:7: "But as for me, I watch in **hope** for the Lord, I wait for God my Savior; my God will hear me." (NIV)
- Romans 15:13: "May the God of **hope** fill you with all joy and peace as you trust in him, so that you may overflow with **hope** by the power of the Holy Spirit." (NIV)
- 1 Corinthians 15:19: "If only for this life we have **hope** in Christ, we are of all people most to be pitied." (NIV)
- Hebrews 10:23: "Let us hold unswervingly to the **hope** we profess, for he who promised is faithful." (NIV)
- Hebrews 11:1: "Now faith is confidence in what we **hope** for and assurance about what we do not see." (NIV)
- 1 Peter 1:3: "Praise be to the God and father of our Lord Jesus Christ! In his great mercy he has given us new birth into a living **hope** through the resurrection of Jesus Christ from the dead." (NIV)

The power of today's Christian music was referenced throughout the previous book that described how Dad thrived during his journey through prostate cancer.

Below is a small sample of songs with powerful lyrics that overflow with hope that is found in a relationship with God:

- "God Really Loves Us" by Crowder in the album "Milk & Honey".
- "Graves into Gardens" - by Elevation Worship & Brandon Lake in the album "Graves into Gardens".
- "It is Well" - by Bethel Music & Kristene Dimarco in the album "You Make Me Brave".

- "Faithful God" - by I AM THEY in the album "Faithful God".
- "Promises" by Maverick City Music & Naomi Raine & Joe L. Barnes in the album "Maverick City Vol. 3 Part 1".
- "All My Hope" by Crowder in the album "American Prodigal".

If you find yourself in a struggle and your "Hope Tank" is nearly depleted, listen to the above songs or find similar songs. There are countless songs available that speak to the Hope we have in Jesus. Take the lyrics to heart and pray for a re-filling of hope. Consider purchasing these or similar songs full of hope and then listen to the songs when times are dark. Listen to them on your way into work, while you are exercising, etc.

It's a dark world. We all could use some hope.

October 30, 2014 (Bruce)

Had my thyroid biopsy this morning and the doctor took 9 samples, all from the same nodule (growth). Not sure that was good news to see that the doctor took so many samples. The doctor had two other doctors also in the room who looked at each sample quickly to determine if there was sufficient quantity of cells. The doctor also asked if I was on a thyroid hormone therapy and the answer was yes. The doctor said that normally slows down or suppresses growth.

November 3, 2014

Today I had my bladder biopsy at around 1:30pm. Recovery was very hard. A lot of pain in the lower stomach area and bladder-felt like I really had to urinate but could not. They gave me two pain killer injections and later a different kind of pain killer. The Dr. did come in and talk to me. I asked the doctor to comment about the possibility whether the samples were cancer. The doctor's bet was that the samples were not cancer. That was good to hear. I pushed the recovery team to get me back to a room so I could go to the restroom; they were trying as fast as possible. However, when I got back to the room no results on trying to go. Also I was very hungry and thirsty so they gave me crackers, and then I asked for more and more. Later I was told that I could not go home until I went to the bathroom. This was almost as bad as my prostate surgery. November 10th is when we meet with the doctor to find out the results.

November 4, 2014

My thyroid biopsy was negative. Great news. So we are now 2 negative biopsies out of 3. One more to go.

November 10, 2014

Well, the honeymoon is over. My bladder biopsy was positive for cancer. It is called a transitional cell cancer or a carcinoma in situ. The cancer cells are found only on the surface of the inner lining of the bladder. It is referred to as State 0. The doctor said it was in the early stages and very treatable.

Treatment options are surgery, chemotherapy, biological therapy, and radiation therapy. Based upon the specific type cancer observed in my bladder, the doctor said biological therapy has been the most effective. In my case it will be six weeks of treatment, once a week, followed by another scope to see if additional treatment or tests are needed. Once the treatment period ends, there are follow-ups with another scope every 3 months. This will last at least a year. There is also another possibility of additional biopsies.

Biological therapy consists of a treatment, which is a liquid containing weakened bacteria. The bacteria help your body's natural defenses (the immune system) to kill cancer cells in the bladder. Liquid is placed in your bladder and you are asked to hold the liquid for a period of time.

I am going to have the treatment done in Florida as they cannot begin it until 3-4 weeks so that the bladder can heal after the biopsy. The doctor will contact the Florida medical facility and provide them with the information.

Side effects are similar to chemotherapy; however, we need to pay particular attention to developing a fever. If that happens, it takes a very strong antibiotic which is given intravenously.

I have no comment at this time on my feelings. It is more like trying to be clinical is a way now to deal with it. Emotions will come later.

November 21, 2014

Just came back from a vacation in Wisconsin. We made reservations after I found out about the bladder cancer-it was an opportunity to get away, or should I say run away. It did not help as every time I go to the bathroom I am reminded about the problem as it still hurts some to urinate toward the end.

I also received a call from the doctor in Florida. My first appointment is scheduled for Dec 9th. I doubt it will be a treatment but instead a meeting with the doctor to determine the best course of action. I am really apprehensive about the treatment. They say you are to hold the liquid in your bladder for 1-2 hours. I don't know how this is possible as it is hard not to regularly go to the bathroom every hour to hour and a half.

This cancer is more frightening than the prostate cancer as they cannot remove the cancer from the bladder, whereas the prostate cancer was removed along with the prostate. I guess they could take the bladder out but that has many complications and not advisable at this time.

How do you go through a stressful time but not give the appearance of being stressful? You really cannot discuss it with anyone as people do not know how to deal with the issue. The tendency is to change the subject. It is like you should "buckle up and get on with it". Many others have it worse than you do. When people find out that it is at an early stage they say that is fortunate. I know they mean well, but really, what is fortunate about having to go through a second major cancer and to wonder if it is going to be ok? Will the treatment be successful, can you endure it with the issues caused by the prostate cancer, how many more hard tests in the future, scopes, biopsies etc? What will be the ramifications from the treatment-more frequent urination stops, more pain, more ??????

December 8, 2014

Today I had my first appointment with the doctor in Florida. I was impressed with the doctor's background and interaction with Donna and myself. The doctor does want to do another Cystoscopy to make sure there is no visible cancer yet in the bladder. Therefore no treatments as of now. The doctor also mentioned that there is a shortage of the immunotherapy drug but that they should have some more in a couple of weeks. The doctor said this is a life time process now as the cancer frequently returns. So there will be a life time process of checks by doing the Cystoscopy.

Public Service Announcement (PSA): Bladder Cancer (Roger)

The word "cystoscopy" will be mentioned many times throughout this book because it is the primary method for doctors to examine the healthiness of the urological process, including the bladder. The word itself doesn't sound too scary, but Dad would be the first one to tell you that the process is not a fun one. Type the word into your favorite search engine to learn about the process. Watching videos about it might not be a good idea. Basically, a cystoscopy is the procedure to insert a camera through the urethra to view the inside of the bladder.

A cystoscopy is the primary method employed when a patient is suffering from bladder cancer. Throughout his 3+ year fight with bladder cancer, Dad went through a plethora of cystoscopies and hated each and every one. But the procedure, no matter how unpleasant, was absolutely necessary if Dad wanted to have a chance at defeating bladder cancer.

Like most cancers, bladder cancer is a significant threat to long life in the United States. Bladder cancer usually starts inside the bladder and is generally treatable when it is detected early and stays inside the bladder. The outlook is challenging when the cancer escapes the bladder and spreads to other parts of the body. Dad's cancer seemed to stay inside his bladder; the doctors never mentioned that it had spread outside the bladder.

The following statistics and information are found on the American Cancer Society website:

- Bladder cancer strikes 80,000 people each year. The cancer is predominantly found in men, but women are not immune. Of the new cases, nearly 75% of the new cases are found in men.
- 90% of the people with bladder cancer are over the age of 55.
- Approximately 17,000 people die from bladder cancer each year. Again, the numbers are higher in men than women: 12,000 men die from bladder cancer each year compared to about 5,000 women.
- As with all cancers, there are risk factors that increase the potential for a person to be afflicted by bladder cancer.
- Treatment options include chemotherapy, radiation, immunotherapy, targeted therapy, and of course, surgery.

While the case rate quantity of bladder cancer is lower than other types of cancer, it is still a disease that, left unchecked, will reduce a person's lifespan, especially if the specific type of cancer is aggressive. As you will read throughout the remainder of the book, Dad's cancer was aggressive.

Here's the PSA: Research the disease and if you are in a risk category, get checked with a doctor. Actually, even if you are not in a high risk category, you may want to check with your doctor. When diagnosed, the only risk categories that Dad fell into was being a male over the age of 55.

The Only Easy Day (Roger)

One of the insults that we learned when we were young was to "stick it where the sun doesn't shine" because we were not yet at the age where the other kids had learned all the colorful adult language.

Dad was about to embark upon a potential lifetime of having doctors put various tools "where the sun doesn't shine" to view and operate on his bladder. Making matters worse, the passageway to the bladder is not intended to have any tools inserted into it, no matter how small or precise the tools are today. At first it was relatively uncomplicated: the doctors inserted a camera into this passageway so that they could detect cancer inside the bladder. But then when cancer was detected, there was another tool inserted that allowed for the scrapping of the cancer cells from the bladder lining. As we will learn later, the last object inserted into this passageway was a chemical to remove the last vestiges of the cancer from the bladder.

Can you imagine doing this procedure multiple times during the year for the rest of your life??? I can't imagine doing it once; in fact, while writing this paragraph, I cringe at the thought of undergoing this procedure. I certainly cannot imagine doing this procedure multiple times per year! Yet that was the reality that Dad was facing due to this latest battle with cancer.

Popular culture tells us that the "only easy day was yesterday". This seems particularly relevant for Dad after he learned of the bladder cancer diagnosis. As with many sayings, there is a lot of truth in those five words.

We live in a fallen and broken world, which is the ultimate source of the pains, stress, sickness, and troubles that we go through on a daily basis. If man wasn't fallen, the saying would be incorrect because every day would be easy.

Don't believe it? Consider examples that we see everyday in nature/Creation. Think of a time when you washed the car outside in the driveway. Assuming the driveway is slanted, as most are, once the water falls off the vehicle, it starts flowing down the driveway towards a drain. If there are obstacles in the way, the water seeks an easier path to flow to the drain. Place a stick in front of the water, and it quickly pushes around the stick to resume it's simple flow to the drain. Electricity is another example: When electric current flows, it seeks the easiest and most direct path to the other material.

It should be of no surprise that the concept of life being difficult is Biblical. Consider the following passage that speaks to the ramification of sin entering the world:

"We know that the whole creation has been groaning as in the pains of childbirth right up to the present time." (Romans 8:22, NIV)

Sin brought pain into the world, upending the perfection of God's Creation. Easy no longer became an option for mankind.

Life is not easy. It wasn't easy for Dad when he was fighting prostate cancer. It definitely wasn't easy for Dad when he was undergoing this procedure in order to fight the bladder cancer. It isn't easy for you as you are struggling today. It won't be easy tomorrow.

But if you continue on with the passage above, there is hope that although tomorrow won't be easy, it will be manageable, especially if we have placed our trust in God:

"Not only so, but we ourselves, who have the firstfruits of the Spirit, groan inwardly as we wait eagerly for our adoption to sonship, the redemption of our bodies. For in this hope we were saved. But hope that is seen is no hope at all. Who hopes for what they already have? But if we hope for what we do not yet have, we wait for it patiently. In the same way, the Spirit helps us in our weakness. We do not know what we ought to pray for, but the Spirit himself intercedes for us through wordless groans. And he who searches our hearts knows the mind of the Spirit, because the Spirit intercedes for God's people in accordance with the will of God. And we know that in all things God works for the good of those who love him, who have been called according to his purpose." (Romans 8:23-28, NIV)

Yes, yesterday was easier than today. But the only truly easy day will be when we are no longer constrained by the sin of this world.

We are not sure when Dad wrote the following poems, but the messages seem relevant for this period of Dad's life. There can be no doubt that he was feeling trapped in this difficult situation that seemingly was never going to end.

Captive (Bruce)

Free to roam, but no more,
Barbed wire fence all around.
Separated from normal,
Contaminated within.
Invisible but so strong,
Eating away, silently.
Racing against time.

How many more laps,
Where does it all lead.
Many hills, many valleys,
Always a fence at the end.
Winding roads, crooked trails,

Tis the season so they say,
To be joyful

Bruce VanderKolk

My Name is Bob (Bruce)

My name is Bob
And I'm getting out.
The gates are locked
The wall is high.
To the other side

I will soon be there;
    For my name is Bob
    And I'm getting out.
Silently walking the hall
    Looking for my prey;
    Stalking, observing, blending
    I'm getting out, for my name is Bob.
Freedom is near
It's just over there;
A resident no more,
I'm getting out, for my name is Bob
See the innocent one
    Never to know,
    Clever that I am
    Foolish they are
    I'm getting out, for my name is Bob
To the other side
    Careful now, the wall is high
    But I can see
    I'm getting out, for my name is Bob.
I move with ease
    Through these quiet halls;
    These halls I've walk
    Here, there, and everywhere
    Always the same
    not much longer
    I'm getting out, for my name is Bob.
Others do not see
    Blind that they are;
    They open the gate
    The chameleon me
    I'm out, for my name is Bob.

Bruce VanderKolk

December 9, 2014 (Bruce)

Had my Cystoscopy this morning at 8:30am. Donna was also in the room watching the screen. The doctor did find that not all of the cancer had been removed. Therefore this doctor speculated that only a biopsy was performed previously. The doctor could see where the biopsy was performed and it is in the same area. Neither doctor have looked at any other area. I am now being scheduled for another surgery to remove the remaining cancer. They call this a TUR. Removal of a tumor during cystoscopy is known as transurethral resection (TUR). Most of the time, tissue removed during TUR can be studied to see if more treatment is needed. They will try to do the surgery next week. Certainly do not look forward to this as last time the recovery was not fun.

Donna and I were discussing that maybe God has had a hand in this as I have encountered a doctor with a lot of experience and in a way it is like a second opinion. What we do not understand at this point is why the first doctor was going immediately to the treatment stage without removing more of the cancer. It does make sense to remove the cancer and then start treatment. Could be just a manner of opinion on how to proceed. Nevertheless it is all in God's hands now as to the outcome. It is nothing that I can influence-I am not in control of this situation. The near term future is not going to be pleasant but God willing the long term future will be good. Maybe He is not done with me yet and has other plans for me. It is hard not to be discouraged but I am sure others have gone through the same process of questioning and asking "Why Me."

At least this time, so far after 4 hours, I do not have the same amount of pain urinating as I did after the last cystoscopy.

2015

A New Year, A New Beginning?? (Roger)

The year 2014 has come and passed. More than likely, Dad was glad to see 2014 in the rear view mirror. He was likely relieved to put that year behind him and look forward to a better 2015. He likely knew that there would be periods of difficulty as he fought against bladder cancer, but he also had high confidence that by the end of 2015 life would return back to normal.

Unfortunately, as you will read, this was not the case.

The Holidays: A Time to Relax

A consistent theme throughout Dad's journaling was that he generally took the last half of December off from writing. In all his journals between the years 2009-2017, there were only a handful of entries from this time period, only three actually.

It seems reasonable to assume that Dad wanted to put aside the journal because the process of writing about his struggles was very "me-centric" which is the opposite mentality that is required for the holiday season. Rather than being down about his station in life, he wanted to enjoy time with family. He wanted to have good, quality, and long-lasting memories with his children, grandchildren, sister-in-law, and brother-in-law.

Another way to look at the holiday break is that, for all practical purposes, the fight against cancer was his full-time job. He quite simply needed a break to rest and recuperate from the fight. This is actually something that he learned in the military: While he was in Vietnam, he was able to take a week of "R&R" time in Hawaii with his new bride. The military recognized the improvement in morale, and consequently fighting condition, by providing a brief respite for their soldiers.

If you're reading this book, the chances are high that you are fighting a battle as well. How about you? Have you taken time lately to rest and recuperate? Is there a holiday coming up on the calendar when you can take some R&R?

I'm not alone with this encouragement; the rock band "The Offspring" agrees as well. There is a brief snippet in the Offspring's album "Smash" that is relevant to this topic. The snippet is called "Time to Relax" and is found wedged among the other songs on the album. Listen to and follow the words of the song to get into the relaxation mode.

January 16, 2015 (Bruce)

Well, surgery was done Jan 12, 2015. I was hooked up to a catheter until Jan 15. Not a pleasant process. Wednesday was not a real good day but things improved Thursday, particularly after the catheter was removed at 7:00am. Today I went for a mile walk and later we went to Family Christian Stores to get a book that a friend recommended called "You'll Get Through This" written by Max Lucado.

When we met with the doctor on Thursday the pathology report was back. All seven areas removed were cancer and it was a fast growing cancer. The doctor also mentioned that there is a worldwide shortage of the bio-therapy treatment that I was going to receive. The doctor did not know when more would be received. The doctor indicated that another doctor in this facility was having patients wait. But my doctor was advising patients to proceed with a chemo treatment. We agreed, and the first treatment is scheduled for Feb 5, 2015. Need to wait a few weeks for the bladder to heal before start treatments. Now I do not know how to evaluate this recent chain of events, e.g. no intended treatment but going directly to chemo. Is this also part of God's plan and will this be the best treatment plan for me?

After six treatments, one per week, then we wait for a couple of weeks and repeat the scope. If cancer remains, there may be a need for another TUR or additional treatments. Possibly by then the treatment will be available.

The Road (Bruce)

I read the book "You'll Get Through This: Hope and Help for Your Turbulent Time" by Max Lucado. Excellent book and very timely for me; some of the key points are outlined below that apply to my situation.

- *Is God good only when the outcome is?*
- *Our choice comes down to this: trust God or turn away. He will cross the line. He will shatter our expectations. And we will be left to make a decision.*
- *"Our light and momentary troubles are achieving for us an eternal glory that far outweighs them all." 2 Cor. 4:17 (NIV)*

I see God in this process in that out of the clear blue my friend called and recommended a book that was just what I needed. Of course the friend knew what I was going through but the timeliness cannot be a coincidence.

The story in the book which follows Joseph prompted me to write the following:

The Road:
All is well, flying on high,
Center of my universe.
But wait, a harsh blow is placed,
And down the pit we now slide.

Jagged edges, slippery slopes,
Falling, falling, how to stop.
Bottom felt; cold, damp, alone,
Universe gone, where is hope?

Voices, voices do you hear?
Hoisted up, shackled and chained.
Options none, must march along,
On the road, filled with great fear.

Trust I must, what else to do,
Surely not to give in now.
Fight, fight with body and mind,
Tis hard; help me to get through.

Road is hard, body is sore,
> Despair is easy, don't stop.
> Onward, upward, forward now,
> Inch by inch; I can take more.

Whatever the conclusion,
> I shall not lose in the end.
> Road of old or road anew,
> Each road is resolution.

James 1:3-4 (NIV) *"because you know that the testing of your faith produces perseverance. 4 Let perseverance finish its work so that you may be mature and complete, not lacking anything."*

2 Corinthians 4:17(NIV) *"For our light and momentary troubles are achieving for us an eternal glory that far outweighs them all."*

January 17, 2015, Bruce W. VanderKolk

(Written after bladder surgery and finding out I have an aggressive bladder cancer. It is still contained in the bladder, however, chemotherapy now awaits and then reevaluation.)

January 21, 2015

I have also started reading Randy Alcorn's book "If God is Good." Reading what others have to say about the presence of God during difficult times has a soothing effect on my emotions.

Last Sunday, Jan 18, 2015, a friend here in Florida mentioned to me about his trials in 1978, 1979, and 1980. He had been diagnosed with pre-cancer of the bladder. He went through 22 months of constant surgeries every 3 months as the pre-cancer kept coming back. Finally it was mentioned to him about taking Vitamin B6. He went on a program of taking massive dosages, 500mg, and it cleared up the pre-cancer. He still takes 50 mg a day but has not had any problems since then.

I looked up on the Internet about it and there have been some studies that Vitamin B6 triggers our immune system and may be effective in fighting bladder *cancer. Some of the studies had a person taking it in conjunction with the treatments I was scheduled to take.*

I emailed the doctor to inquire about it. I received a call from a nurse who said it would be ok but should be taken with other vitamins. Later I received an email from the doctor which said: "Dear Mr. VanderKolk, Thank you for contacting us. Absolutely, taking those supplements is a great idea. See you soon and we will discuss the topic again. Thank you.

I am currently taking 100mg once a day in the evening until I can further discuss with the doctor.

(Author's Note: Reminder that neither Bruce nor the author are qualified to dispense any medical advice. The above is simply a recording of Bruce's research and subsequent action for his situation. This behavior should not be construed as a treatment plan for anyone reading this book. If you have questions, please consult your medical professional.)

February 6, 2015 (Bruce)

I have upped my dosage of Vitamin B6 to 100mg in the morning and 100mg in the evening. The doctor said that was ok. The doctor also suggested I take a supplemental vitamin that had a small amount of vitamin B6 plus other vitamins.

Yesterday, February 5, 2015, I had my first chemo treatment at 1:00p. I basically stopped drinking after supper the night before as you are to hold the chemo in your bladder for 2 hours, rotating on your sides, back and stomach every 10-15 minutes. I call it self-dehydration. I made the 2 hours but the last five minutes were hard because of bladder spasms.

The doctor has provided a lot of information on the treatment, which I have summarized below:

Intravesical chemotherapy — Chemotherapy refers to the use of medicines to stop or slow the growth of cancer cells. The most commonly used intravesical chemotherapy for bladder cancer is the one I am taking. This is put inside the bladder in one of two ways:

- *One regimen involves giving the chemotherapy once, immediately after TURBT. The solution is left in the bladder for 30 to 60 minutes, then allowed to drain out through a catheter.*

- Alternately, the chemotherapy can be given on a weekly basis for six weeks. With this regimen, the bladder is filled with the chemotherapy with a catheter, the solution is left for one to two hours, then the person urinates. A maintenance treatment may be given once per month for up to one year.
- I am on the six weeks program. The treatment of choice is not available because of a world wide shortage.
- The chemotherapy is also used to treat a variety of other cancers but it is injected into the blood system and can cause hair loss.
- The following explains other uses: Used in combination with other medications to treat cancer of the stomach or pancreas that has spread to other parts of the body and has not improved or worsened after treatment with other medications, surgery, or radiation therapy.
- It is a type of antibiotic that is only used in cancer chemotherapy. It slows or stops the growth of cancer cells in your body.

The treatment was not as bad as I expected and have had only minor issues, namely more frequent urination. I must say the process of applying the chemo is not the most pleasant experience. The potential side effects include:

- Often causes temporary irritation of the bladder, including the need to urinate frequently and urgently and pain with urination.
- Can also cause a skin rash on the palms of the hands, soles of the feet, and genitals. If this rash occurs, treatment needs to be stopped and should not be restarted. Occasionally steroid therapy is prescribed if the effects are severe and not resolving on their own. A different chemotherapy drug or even the treatment might be substituted in this situation.
- Rarely, the chemotherapy can cause the bladder to shrink down so that it holds less urine.

I was able to go out to the store after the two hours. Today we went to several places-just need to make sure I can get to a restroom as the urge becomes strong with bladder spasms.

February 14, 2015
On Thursday I had my second chemo treatment. Again I was able to hold the chemo for the required two hours but the last 10 minutes were really

uncomfortable and at times painful. The cramps or spasms became frequent and hard. I almost quit with 5 minutes to go but I so badly wanted to make the two hours I just gutted it out.

The after-effects were somewhat more intense than before. I still developed a slight headache which lasted until about 8:00pm. It also seemed that the spasms were harder after urination then before. Fortunately they only last from 5 to 10 seconds. Today, the 14th, I have only had a few spasms and they were not as intense. I have also been finding out that the ability to hold urine is really hard and one must get to the bathroom ASAP. I am wondering if part of this is also due to the pain medicine they insert so that the catheter and injection of the chemo is not as painful as it might be. Possibly the pain medicine until it wears off makes control of the muscles more difficult.

My vitamin regimen has arrived and I have started taken them. It does give me an additional 100 mg of Vitamin B-6. This raises my dosage to 300 mg. It calls for taking two tablets but I only take one a day as I did not want to get to the 400 mg of Vitamin B-6. The tablet also contains a host of other vitamins to include a large amount of vitamin A. I have read that vitamin A also helps in treatment of bladder cancer.

After the six treatments I have been scheduled for another scope on April 8, 2015. This will reveal whether or not the chemo is working and has been successful or only partially successful.

I continue to be amazed at the number of cards I receive and people asking how I am doing plus all of those who are praying for me during this ordeal. It means a lot.

Leaning on Friends (Roger)

The concept of finding a "Battle Buddy" to assist in periods of struggle was discussed in the previous book. During his battle with prostate cancer, Dad was blessed to be in a position where he could share his experience and learn from others that had gone through a similar battle.

There is another dynamic found in some of our relationships with other people: Sometimes we just need people to be present and to simply be in the moment with us. We need people that are there to listen to our struggles, doubts, and questions. We need people that are not involved with our struggle but are there to visit with us. We need people that will answer the phone when we call.

Dad was beyond blessed in this area. He had many people across the country that would either call him or pick up the phone when he called because he needed someone not fighting cancer to chat. People such as Marvin VanderKolk (Brother), Gary Knight, Dave Jackson, Dean Hughes, Alice Ransler, Jim Jacobs, Lindy Moore, Lee Ossmann, Betty Browning, Bob Crites, Larry Scheufele, and Jim Northrup.

(There are many more names not in the previous paragraph. The author apologizes for neglecting friends who played an important role in Dad's life while he was fighting cancer. However, this just goes to show, the level of character by which Dad lived his life. He had friends everywhere.)

By and large these friends were people of faith which made any conversation about life or death easier because they had the same starting point: confidence that the forever outcome of this life is favorable.

There are three men that held a special place in Dad's heart:

1. James VanderKolk - Beloved son of Bruce. Their relationship really blossomed and strengthened when Mom and Dad moved to the same small town in northern Illinois where James lived with his family. And not only did Mom and Dad move to the same town, they moved into the house immediately next door to James and his family! James was constantly available throughout Dad's struggle with prostate and bladder cancer. It was such a blessing from God that they were able to spend that much time together. Both of them were blessed. Their closeness was such that James actually asked Dad to be his best man for his wedding ceremony.

2. Jeff Chitwood - Dad's relationship with Jeff started the moment Jeff became the Youth Minister at South Side Christian Church in Springfield, IL. Early in his ministry, Jeff asked Mom and Dad to get involved with the youth. Their relationship was strengthened when Jeff became the Senior Minister for the church because Dad was a constant presence on the Board of Elders. When Dad retired from the Illinois State Police, he went to work at the church as the Administrator and his relationship with Jeff grew even

stronger. When Jeff moved to a church in Florida, my parents eventually ended up moving to the same city and Dad went back to working alongside Jeff. Throughout the decades there were countless lunch meetings, many family dinners together, and hundreds, if not thousands, of phone calls. Dad was a mentor to Jeff but Jeff was also a mentor to Dad as well.

3. Donald Aulbert - Don, as the kids would say, was Dad's "brother from another mother". Don was married to Mom's sister so he and Bruce were, for lack of a better word, "forced" into a relationship. But there again, God took a situation and turned it into a blessing. Dad and Don became very close friends throughout their 40 years of relationship. A skilled carpenter and all around handyman, Don was the teacher while Dad was the willing apprentice. Together they built dozens of projects, made countless trips to the hardware store to purchase items they had originally forgotten, and even a few trips to the emergency room when a construction project went bad. The two couples took many vacation trips together, including several cruises to the Caribbean. They spent thousands of hours together and basically became brothers. Dad leaned on Don a lot, not only to increase his project knowledge, but also to increase his faith in God as well.

How about you? Which friends in your life will pick up the phone when you call, no matter the time of day? Friends that will chat with you about the latest sports score or rant about politics? Friends that will listen to the frustrations about your struggle. Friends that will discuss the weather or latest crop report.

But there is more to this than you leaning on friends for your support. How many friends would consider you that type of friend? How many people in your life would you answer the phone for if they called in the middle of the night? Is that list long or is it a short list? If the list is short, you might want to pick up the phone and start calling people yourself so that they will be able to lean on you.

This is another dichotomy about life: We need people to lean on during our struggle and we need to be there for others when they are struggling.

March 2, 2015 (Bruce)

Last Thurs, Feb 26, 2015, I had my fourth chemo treatment. I lasted a couple of minutes beyond the two hours required to retain the chemo liquid.

I am not sure why, but I have had no after-effects from this treatment such as the bladder spasms or quick urge to "go". It seems that the first treatment was the worst and each one following has been a little better.

Is this good news or bad news? Does this mean the chemo is not working and therefore no bladder irritation or has it been successful and most of the cancer is gone? I need to ask this week when I go in for my 5th treatment.

March 6, 2015

Five treatments down and one more to go. Again, no aftereffects. I asked about that and the nurse did not know: everyone reacts differently. Some have problems at beginning and some later, or a combination of other side effects. The nurse always asks if I had any pain with last treatment, fever, joint soreness, rash, etc. I still believe that it is a positive sign that I am no longer having bladder spasms. That would imply to me that the chemo is not encountering any cancer cells on the lining of the bladder. Again, I lasted the full two hours.

Elephants and Manageable Goals (Roger)

The last sentence of Dad's previous journal entry brings to mind a well-known metaphor: "How do you eat an elephant? One bite at a time."

Dad's situation is no different than anyone else who is facing an impossible situation or task. The tendency is to panic at the thought of having to do everything all at once in order to succeed or survive. But the solution is to break down the major task into manageable sub-tasks which are easier to accomplish. Being able to successfully complete these smaller tasks not only creates progress towards the ultimate goal, but it also improves morale because there is progress being made. It reduces the overwhelming sense of powerlessness.

Dad couldn't eliminate the cancer that was growing in his bladder. Dad couldn't control the effectiveness of the treatment at reducing the cancer spots in his bladder. Dad couldn't control the amount of times that he had to relieve himself in the bathroom during a typical day.

But he recognized that he could control the length of time that he held the treatment in his bladder. So what did he do? He focused on hitting the two hour time mark with each treatment. Did it truly make a difference in the effectiveness of the treatment? Perhaps. But perhaps not: It's not unreasonable to think that having the treatment in the bladder for 1 hour and 55 minutes would be inferior than having it in the bladder for the two hours. But it was important to Dad to hit the two hour mark so that he could see progress in his fight against the bladder cancer.

There's actually an example of this process in the Bible. In Genesis 6, the Bible records that God had decided to wipe mankind from the earth because of their great wickedness. He did find a family that was worthy of saving though: a man called Noah, his sons, and their wives. Noah was instructed to build an ark in order to escape the coming flood:

> "So God said to Noah, 'I am going to put an end to all people, for the earth is filled with violence because of them. I am surely going to destroy both them and the earth. So make yourself an ark of cypress wood; make rooms in it and coat it with pitch inside and out. This is how you are to build it: The ark is to be three hundred cubits long, fifty cubits wide and thirty cubits high. Make a roof for it, leaving below the roof an opening one cubit high all around. Put a door in the side of the ark and make lower, middle and upper decks. I am going to bring floodwaters on the earth to destroy all life under the heavens, every creature that has the breath of life in it. Everything on earth will perish. But I will establish my covenant with you, and you will enter the ark—you and your sons and your wife and your sons' wives with you. You are to bring into the ark two of all living creatures, male and female, to keep them alive with you. Two of every kind of bird, of every kind of animal and of every kind of creature that moves along the ground will come to you to be kept alive. You are to take every kind of food that is to be eaten and store it away as food for you and for them.'" (Genesis 6:13-21, NIV)

There are a few items here for consideration. First, the ark described above is huge, about the size of a modern day cruise ship. There wasn't a team of hundreds of builders and workers, there was only Noah and his family. Talk about a gigantic project! It must have been completely overwhelming. The Bible doesn't record it, but we must assume that Noah tackled the ark one sub-project at a time. Second, there is no mention of rain in the Bible prior to the flood. God was asking Noah to build a boat to float on water that would magically come from the sky. Noah didn't question it; because of his faith, he got to work building the ark. We should strive to have faith like Noah.

Back to that huge task in front of you. What do you need to do in order to have elephant for dinner (IE: complete the project)?

(Not literally. Please don't go out and kill and eat an elephant.)

March 25, 2015 (Bruce)

DONE! Now we wait for the 8th of April for another scope to see how effective the chemo treatments have been. The urine test today was pristine. The nurse said no trace of blood and all the numbers were perfect. This makes me wonder when I went to the medical facility for prostate tests and they kept finding a small amount of blood if this wasn't due to the Bladder Cancer starting before I had the flakes. If so, then maybe the doctor should have pursued this more than just shrugging it off or contributing it to biking. It would be interesting to know how long I had the Bladder Cancer. Possibly when I had the pain in urinating for a few years after exercising a lot was because the cancer was starting? Made it again for the full two hours.

April 8, 2015

Good report from the scope. The doctor did not see any visible signs of the cancer. Praise God. Go back July 1, 2015, for a three month evaluation.

Secondary Mission (Roger)

If you are in the midst of a struggle against a serious illness, your number one mission right now is to fight the battle while still blessing the lives of those around you. That is your primary mission. But what about a secondary mission? What is your secondary mission?

What is a secondary mission, you ask? Something that is important to you, gets you out of bed in the morning, and takes your mind off of your primary mission. This goes beyond a "passion project". The secondary mission is a cause, something that will leave your mark on the world around you.

Dad had many secondary missions throughout the years of his struggles. These revolved around his church, whether it was the church in downstate Illinois, northern Illinois, or Southwestern Florida. He wanted to use his experiences, gifts, and capabilities to make the churches a more welcoming place for newcomers. He wanted to reach out to those without a relationship with God who were also in a seeking phase of life. These missions were significant because they had eternal consequences.

From an earthly perspective, his most significant secondary mission was the improvement and transformation of the memorial to fallen soldiers located in downtown Oregon, IL. Dad and Mom had moved to the area to be nearer to their son and grandchildren. As a retired Brigadier General, Dad was one of the highest ranking armed forces members in the area. He became a member of the local VFW chapter and observed with dismay the neglected condition of the existing memorial. He believed the fallen soldiers deserved better and launched a campaign to create a new memorial.

The new VFW memorial campaign started from scratch and thus occupied a lot of Dad's time and energy. He spent countless hours in front of the computer sending emails to donors, working with a local artist on a new sculpture for the memorial, talking on the phone to the various committee members, as well as a host of other activities. This work gave him purpose. It also kept his mind off the fight with bladder cancer.

The crowning event was a giant fund-raiser held on May 16, 2015. The next section is an email, dated March 2, 2015, that he sent to potential donors for the fund-raiser. In the email Dad describes the importance of this memorial to not only the families of the fallen soldiers, but also to the community as a whole. Over 100 people from the surrounding community attended the event to raise money for the new memorial.

It should come as no surprise therefore that Dad accomplished this secondary mission. The new VFW memorial was dedicated during the Veteran's Day observance in November, 2015. On a cold and blustery day, despite all of the pain from the various bladder treatments, Bruce donned his dress uniform, gave a speech, and dedicated the memorial to those who made the ultimate sacrifice for their country. The memorial continues to provide an opportunity to remember those personnel to this day.

Throughout the project, Dad participated in the following activities that surely provided a needed distraction from his struggles:

- Formulated the idea of a new, vibrant memorial
- Led the planning process
- Secured project approval from the local authorities
- Developed a fund raising campaign
- Led the fund-raising campaign
- Ensured community involvement with an official dedication ceremony

Your secondary mission doesn't have to be as large of an effort as Dad's. He would be the first to tell you that he just happened to be in the right place at the right time and was blessed to be able to use his unique gifts to turn the project into a reality.

But you need to have some sort of a secondary mission. Perhaps it is just something as simple as helping out with the local homeless shelter or pet shelter. Whatever it is, use your time to help others, while at the same time taking your mind off your current struggle.

Do you have a secondary mission? If so, what is your secondary mission? If not, do some thinking and identify 2-3 possibilities. Remember: Your secondary mission doesn't have to be world-changing; it just has to provide a sense of purpose for you and those around you.

Below is the email that Dad sent to various members of the community to solicit donations for the new memorial. The content of the email shows how important the memorial was to Dad, even in the midst of his fight against bladder cancer.

———————————————————————

Who Will Remember? (Bruce)

Last fall on a cold day in Oregon, I was at the Ogle County Veterans Memorial which pays tribute to those who have given their lives for our country since WWI. As I was standing at the Memorial, a teacher with several grade school children came up to observe the memorial. As I watched from a distance, I wondered what the teacher was telling the children. Was she explaining:

- The meaning behind the Memorial; or,
- Did she recognize some names on the plaque; or,
- What it means to have served in the military and to be a veteran; or,
- The personal sacrifice of giving one's life for their country; or,
- Why it is important to have a Memorial to honor our Fallen Soldiers?

What was her motivation to bring school children to the memorial?

- Was she attempting to instill a sense of gratefulness for our Fallen Soldiers;
- Was she using this as an example that freedom is not free,
- Was she using the example of the past sacrifices to forge an example of patriotic duty?

At the same time I wondered what was going through the minds of the children.

- Did they understand when they saw names such as: Earl Bender, Thomas Koritz, Ralyn M. Hill, Patrick Manning, John Page, or,
- Were they overwhelmed by the many names, or,
- Did they fully understand how the loss of a soldier impacted family, friends, community, or,
- Did it instill a sense of appreciation and awareness that this country remains free as well as other countries because of personal sacrifice?

As I think about that cold, fall day at the Oregon Courthouse Square, I am grateful for the teacher's willingness to take her classroom to the Memorial. But I must ask the question: if there is no Memorial, what will be there for future generations to remember our "Fallen Soldiers?"

The current Memorial has been repaired once and is in need of repair again and plaques replaced. If we as veterans do not lead the effort to construct a new and appropriate Memorial, WHO WILL? Will the current Memorial continue to disintegrate and be a shameful tribute to those who sacrificed their lives? I do not want to see that happen, do you?

We need your support. If you have not purchased a paver to honor our "Fallen Soldiers" please do so. I also urge you to register for the May 16th, 2015, Armed Forces Day celebration at Barnacopia. Major General Boring, our speaker, endured 6 years and 8 months as a POW at the Hanoi Hilton. His story is inspiring. Thank you.

Bruce VanderKolk, Vietnam Veteran, March 2, 2015

June 25, 2015 (Bruce)

Well, it is a concept of going forward and then going backward. Hopefully the forward motion is greater than the backward motion. I had my cystoscope today and the doctor saw three small red areas to be concerned about. Consequently I am scheduled for a biopsy of these areas on Monday, June 29, 2015, at a local medical facility. If negative good. If positive, then we are back to repeating the process, e.g. surgery, and then treatments.

I am not surprised. The doctor has frequently mentioned I had an aggressive form of cancer. The good news is that we have gone from seven areas to three and none of the three had the cauliflower appearance. However, a red area could be the beginning stages of the cancer. Last time I had the cauliflower appearance and flaking of the site into the urine.

I would like to say I have a very good attitude and everything is nice and rosy. I cannot make that statement. I am getting tired of seeing doctors and constantly being concerned about the cancers I have. I particularly do not like the procedures I must go through either for the cystoscope, surgery or chemo treatments.

On a positive note, my PSA came back at 0.00 which means there is no prostate cancer at this point in my body.

I told Donna if my cancer is still present, I want to run away from everything. But where would I go? I guess I need to be told "just suck it up." It *is easy for this situation to kill one's initiative and I would like to say "pi—off" but instead I respond with a lie and say good when people ask how I am doing. I know people are simply concerned and that is appreciated but it is also hard being hypocritical. No one really wants to hear you spill your guts, so you go on as if everything in the world couldn't be better.*

Coupled with this issue is that for a month or so I have been bothered with a dislike for most foods and nausea at night after supper. I think this is from an increase dosage in my medicine for diabetes. The Dr raised my medicine from 1000mg a day at night to 2000mg.

June 29, 2015

Went for my biopsy today at a local medical facility. Appointment was 10:20 and got back into the room at around 11:10. Almost ready to get prep for cystoscope biopsy and electricity went off. After 20 min it was decided to come back June 30th at 6:30am. At least I wasn't half way through the procedure.

June 30, 2015

Got up at 4:45am and got to the medical facility about 6:20am. Had the biopsy done and the doctor took three samples: two from one area and one sample from a second area. The doctor had mentioned previously that samples would not be pulled from the third area-if the first two were positive then so was the third. But if they were negative, so was the third.

I was surprised that the doctor took two from one area. The doctor had not mentioned this previously. I think the suspicion is that the samples are positive, at least the one where the doctor took two samples. The doctor wants to see me again on August 10th-this is as soon as we can be back in Florida because of Donna's cataract surgery. I should know next week if it is positive.

As far as the procedure, it was not the most pleasant but could have been worse. The worst part after the doctor removed the samples was the cauterizing of the areas. Not fun. I am pleasantly surprised that I have had no problems urinating today. The biopsy done in Illinois was the worst time I have ever had in the recovery room and pain afterwards for a couple of days urinating.

We went back to the condo and left for Illinois. Ok as far as driving went. The doctor did want me to stop and go to the bathroom about every hour to prevent the bladder to fill up and stretch the bladder because of the cauterized areas.

AN ENRICHING EXPERIENCE (Bruce)

Allison was her name.

I do not know his name.

She was a waitress,

He was a homeless person.

We were participants with them in a live trilogy of life. We all had different backgrounds, different walks of life, but we were all brought together unexpectedly. Strangers, but now linked to a shared experience never to be separated.

The Story:

As we walked up to a Bob Evans restaurant, there he was sitting on the sidewalk. He had a few possessions but not many. His face was wrinkled, his clothes were ragged, and he had that beaten downcast expression; it was obvious he had not had a bath in a few or several days. Maybe he was in his 60's but who could tell.

My wife and I took a seat at a table and we discussed the homeless person and his plight. Should we offer to buy him dinner or not. Have you ever been in a similar situation after encountering a homeless person? Soon Allison came over to take our order. We asked Allison if the man outside was a homeless person and she said yes. Apparently he was well known to the employees. We asked if he would accept a meal. Allison said he probably would not, because he does not accept money, etc, as he is a proud man and refuses handouts. We asked Allison if she would mind asking him if we could buy him a meal. She said yes, and shortly came back with a surprised look on her face saying he had accepted. The man came into the restaurant and sat on the other side, out of our vision.

Our story started out to help a homeless person. But we soon realized that Allison was touched more by the act of kindness than we could have imagined. With glossy eyes she said it did her heart good to think that we would help a homeless person. She asked if we lived in the area and we said no, we were just passing through.

Our lives were impacted, not so much because of the homeless person, but because of the emotional impact the "act of kindness" had upon Allison. It was obvious that she was emotionally impacted and had a heart for others. Words alone cannot describe how we saw Allison impacted; nor do words alone describe how our hearts were touched.

Linked together for a moment but now linked together forever. An opportunity presented, an opportunity taken. Thank you Anchor Christian Church for your message of Love God, Love our neighbors, by being the hands, feet, and heart of Jesus.

Bruce W. VanderKolk
June 30, 2015

July 8, 2015 (Bruce)

They say no news is good news. Well today I received news from the doctor and my biopsy was positive for bladder cancer. The same type of bladder cancer as before. So it is back to Florida for surgery August 17, 2015, and followed by treatments. The doctor said hopefully there would be a sufficient amount of the treatment by then to use. This is the same drug used for a vaccine of another disease.

The surgery will involve again scrapping the area where the cancer is located and then the treatments. I was not surprised as the Dr. seemed to give clues that there was concern about one of the areas that had a biopsy, like taking two samples from one area. Plus when I called on Monday for the result I was told they do not give results over the phone. If it is negative what difference does it make? But if it is positive, then I can see where the Dr would want to meet with the patient. Anyway, I asked for the Dr to call me as I could not drive to Florida just to get the results.

Jamie asked how I felt. I said I was mad and disgusted. He asked who I was mad at and I said no one specifically, just mad in general. It would be nice to go at least 12 months without any problems.

Below is some information on bladder cancer stage definitions and 5-year survival rates that seem to be common knowledge because they are found on multiple online sites. The doctor who did the first biopsy said I had a stage 1 cancer. I need to confirm with the current doctor if that is indeed his opinion as well.

In general, for bladder cancer, the following is used to classify the stages:

- *Stage 0: Cancer stays in the inner lining*
- *Stage 1: Cancer has spread to the bladder wall*
- *Stage 2: Cancer has reached the muscle of the bladder wall*

- Stage 3: Cancer has spread to fatty tissue around the bladder
- Stage 4: Cancer has spread to the pelvic or abdominal wall, lymph nodes, or distant sites such as bone, liver, etc.

Survival rates are often used by doctors as a standard way of discussing a person's prognosis (outlook). Some people with cancer may want to know the survival statistics for people in similar situations, while others may not find the numbers helpful, or may even not want to know them.

(If you would rather not read the survival rates for bladder cancer, skip to the next section.)

The 5-year survival rate refers to the percentage of patients who live at least 5 years after their cancer is diagnosed. Of course, many people live much longer than 5 years (and many are cured). Five-year relative survival rates assume that some people will die of other causes and compare the observed survival with that expected for people without the cancer. This is a more accurate way to describe the chances of dying from a particular type and stage of cancer.

In order to get 5-year survival rates, doctors have to look at people who were treated at least 5 years ago. Improvements in treatment since then may result in a better outlook for people now being diagnosed with bladder cancer.

The numbers below are based on thousands of people diagnosed with bladder cancer from 1988 to 2001 and reflect a Relative 5-year Survival Rate. These numbers come from the National Cancer Institute's SEER database:

- Stage 0: 98%
- Stage 1: 88%
- Stage 2: 63%
- Stage 3: 46%
- Stage 4: 15%

Survival rates are often based on previous outcomes of large numbers of people who had the disease, but they can't predict what will happen. Knowing the type and the stage of a person's cancer is important in estimating their outlook. But many other factors can also affect a person's outlook, such as other health problems, the grade of the cancer, and how well the cancer responds to treatment. Your doctor can tell you how the numbers above apply to you.

August 5, 2015

When they are down, kick them harder to keep them down.

That is what it felt like today when I saw the doctor for a three month checkup on my diabetes and thyroid reading. The doctor went over the readings and all was ok except the TSH reading of 17 (and previously 11 at the VA in July) was way too low.

The doctor proceeded to tell me I needed an MRI brain scan to check out to see if there are any growths on the pituitary gland. A tumor can cause a reduced reading. Well this certainly came out of the blue and was like a kick in the stomach.

I could not get my test scheduled before we left for Florida for my surgery so it is now scheduled for November 16, 2015, at a local medical facility.

Outward Mentality (Roger)

The next five pages of Dad's journal are dedicated to all the information he could find related to pituitary tumors: symptoms, hormone level changes, the different types of tumors and impact on the body, causes, complications, etc. For hours he would be in his den, scouring the Internet on his computer to learn more about the life-altering condition that the doctor informed he potentially could be facing. He wanted to find out as much as possible to gain an advantage over this latest medical condition.

There is little doubt that the impetus for the research was to be fully prepared if there was a fight against another disease looming on the horizon. But the inclusion of this information into his journal speaks to the importance in his mind of helping others in the same situation. He wanted to share his newfound knowledge with others that might not have the same access to the Internet or the time required to conduct all this research.

One of the main thrusts of the first book bears repeating: In order to Thrive, we must look outside of ourselves and our circumstances. Yes, it is important to focus on our journey and struggle so that we can do everything possible to come out on the other side victorious. But as we focus on others, we increase their chances of a successful journey by giving them additional tools to aid their fight. Focusing on others also helps us by taking our minds off the current struggle, if only for a short time.

How can you focus outwardly?

- First, recognize that there are others worse off than you. If you slept indoors last night, recognize that there are many who either didn't sleep indoors or had to sleep someplace other than a home of their own. Is the disease you're fighting taking a toll on you today? Recognize that you woke up this morning and are reading this book.
- Identify someone specific that could use some assistance. Perhaps it is the co-worker who is struggling to care for an elderly parent or relative. Perhaps it is the cashier you see every morning while ordering your daily cup of coffee. Struggling people are out there; you just have to open your eyes.
- Think about what you can do to assist with improving another person's life (this would be a great opportunity to pray if that is something you are comfortable with doing). Create a list.
- Execute. Do the list. Focus on that person. Put yourself and your trials behind you for just a few moments today.

Who in your life can you allocate some time to go and to visit? Who can you call on the phone and be a friend that they can lean on?

_____

August 10, 2015 (Bruce)

Saw the doctor this morning and it was not the most encouraging meeting. My cancer is an aggressive cancer and has a 40% chance of returning after a treatment. So I am in the 40% group. The doctor will try surgery again to scrap as much of the cancer as possible and then proceed with the treatments. I do not think I will get the desired treatment because of the limited supply and probably will get chemotherapy agent again although the doctor would not say for sure.

If the cancer returns again after the second surgery and treatment the doctor will probably refer me to a different medical facility for further treatment possibilities, one of which is removal of the bladder. However, that would be a last resort. The goal is to not have the cancer break through the wall of the bladder and enter the system to spread.

I mentioned to him about the possibility of reconstructing a new bladder and the doctor said because of my prostate removal after prostate cancer I am not a good candidate. There is a potential of urine leakage and then the need to wear a diaper. The better alternative (if there is a good alternative) is to remove the bladder and then have an external bag.

My only hope for the future is that this surgery works and the treatment works. Otherwise the future is looking bleak, certainly in terms of quality of life.

The procedure for removing the bladder is called "Cystectomy". Afterwards you will need to have a bag taped to your stomach.

August 21, 2015

Well I had my surgery August 17, 2015, at 2:00pm. Lasted about 1 hour and then in recovery I had the chemo treatment. This was very unpleasant and hurt even after the drug was removed from the bladder. Did take a painkiller and got an order for more. Not a very pleasant evening or night. Slept on the recliner chair. Had a leg cath in so had to get up periodically to empty that. Visiting nurse came and took vitals, etc.

Next day had a new visiting nurse and the nurse left me with a large cath container that I could use at night. Slept in the bed. At least I did not need to get up. Day was just so-so.

Drinking a lot of liquids. Over 4000ml a day. But I was told I needed to keep the bladder flushed out.

On Thursday, the visiting nurse came and took out the cath. That is a relief. Jamie left about 11:20am for home. Donna took him to the Punta Gorda airport. I did not go as I still wasn't feeling well and with all that liquid I had to pee about every 15-20 minutes.

Today is Friday and we walked a mile and went out to breakfast at Perkins. It was ok.

I think this recovery is taking longer than the first surgery. Not sure. Wednesday next week we see the surgeon and find out path results as well as next step.

August 26, 2015

The roller coaster ride continues, up/down/sideways and every way. This morning I saw the doctor about what is next as far as treatment. The doctor is recommending me to a dedicated cancer facility that has a pretty good ranking.

The doctor wants a second opinion about what would be best. The doctor also believes they may have access to the preferred treatment. The doctor's goal is to treat the cancer and not have to remove the bladder.

My two biopsies revealed the following:

- Denuded urothelial mucosa (no detrusor muscle present) sample-bladder, dome,
- Urothelial carcinoma in situ (no detrusor muscle present) sample-bladder, posterior.

Also mentioned on the pathology report was a statement that immunohistochemical staining for CK 20 is noncontributory.

Transitional cell or urothelial carcinoma is the most common type of bladder cancer, accounting for more than 90% of all bladder cancers. Urothelial carcinomas are separated clinically into superficial tumors and muscle invasive tumors.

September 11, 2015

Today I saw a doctor at the medical facility. The doctor was young and seemed very sharp. The doctor is going to have a CT scan done on Monday September 14, 2015, and then I have my first treatment there at the same facility. I am going to get the preferred treatment this time and will actually stay at the facility for the two hours rather than leave like I did with the other treatment. This could have some adverse side effects after the 4th treatment and on. About 50-60% of the patients experience some type of problem. I will have six treatments for six weeks and then wait for six weeks to have another scope (December 2, 2015). Depending on the results, I may go on maintenance after 3 months with three additional treatments and continue for awhile or if this does not work there is another chemo drug but it is only about 20% effective.

Obviously we are on a very long process. The doctor said my cancer is stage 1 and has not gone out of the wall but it is a very aggressive cancer. We talked briefly about having the bladder removed and options.

September 17, 2015

On September 15th, at 8:00am, I had a CT scan with contrast dye. The purpose is to make sure it has not spread to any other areas.

At 1:30pm I had my first treatment at the medical facility. This is a large place where I had the treatment. After the prep, it wasn't until 3:00 before they could give me the treatment. I was able to hold it for the full two hours but the last 30 minutes was difficult.

They have three valet/entrances. We entered at the "gold" entrance. It was like being at a fair waiting for a ride - four rows of cars arriving and waiting to be parked and about three rows of cars leaving after patients were ready to leave. All of these people are cancer patients. There were many who were much worse off than myself. A lot in wheel chairs. Some were very thin, some pale, and many who were just existing. I do not know how someone could work at a cancer center and deal with this everyday realizing that many of the patients will not make it. These workers inspire me daily.

The facility was large and had rooms around a large nursing station. I had my own private room with TV which helped. Donna was able to sit in the room. All of the nurses and staff were very nice and accommodating. After the treatment we went back to the hotel as I had to put bleach in the toilet every time I went for six hours. Did not finish that process until 11:00am. Other than once-in-awhile pain in the bladder after I go, there has been no other side affects at this time.

Next treatment September 22, 2015. We will go up Monday and leave Wednesday. We have a suite at a nearby hotel. Monday through Thursday they also serve an evening meal. So with a free breakfast and dinner it is very reasonable.

Saints Among Us (Roger)

"I do not know how someone could work at a cancer center and deal with this everyday realizing that many of the patients will not make it."

There are a lot of very smart people that work at this particular medical facility, people that could very easily find a job at a non-cancer medical facility. But these people made the conscious decision to work at this medical facility because they wanted to help people, such as Dad, be successful in their fight against cancer. Thinking back to that medical facility, this type of calling was typified in every paid employee and volunteer. From the time that Mom and Dad entered that facility, the amount of mercy, grace, and compassion they were shown truly made a positive impact on Dad's struggle with bladder cancer.

Another way to look at these people is that working at this medical facility is their calling. Being in a position to provide comfort for others is their purpose while on this earth. These workers wake up, every morning, and choose to work with people that are facing serious illnesses. They may even have to deal with death on a regular basis. But yet, they still choose to help people. These workers assist patients by the hundreds, if not thousands, and are truly saints walking among us.

All of us have been created for a specific purpose (or purposes) by God. Have you discovered your purpose yet? Perhaps you have been called to work or volunteer at a similar medical facility and have put it off because you're scared. It is a sacred responsibility for us on this earth to give back and to work with those less fortunate than ourselves. Even if we are feeling extremely bad, there are always people worse off than us. It is our calling to help those people.

Finding this purpose in life is important if you are a non-believer, but is critical if you are a born-again believer in the one true God. The following portion from the book of Matthew clearly communicates our responsibility at helping others:

Matthew 25: 31-46 (NIV):
"When the Son of Man comes in his glory, and all the angels with him, he will sit on his glorious throne. All the nations will be gathered before him, and he will separate the people one from another as a shepherd separates the sheep from the goats. He will put the sheep on his right and the goats on his left.

'Then the King will say to those on his right, 'Come, you who are blessed by my Father, take your inheritance, the kingdom prepared for you since the creation of the world. For I was hungry and you gave me something to eat, I was thirsty and you gave me something to drink, I was a stranger and you invited me in, I needed clothes and you clothed me, I was sick and you looked after me, I was in prison and you came to visit me.'

'Then the righteous will answer him, 'Lord, when did we see you hungry and feed you, or thirsty and give you something to drink? When did we see you a stranger and invite you in, or needing clothes and clothe you? When did we see you sick or in prison and go to visit you?'

'The King will reply, 'Truly I tell you, whatever you did for one of the least

of these brothers and sisters of mine, you did for me.'

'Then he will say to those on his left, 'Depart from me, you who are cursed, into the eternal fire prepared for the devil and his angels. For I was hungry and you gave me nothing to eat, I was thirsty and you gave me nothing to drink, I was a stranger and you did not invite me in, I needed clothes and you did not clothe me, I was sick and in prison and you did not look after me.'

'They also will answer, 'Lord, when did we see you hungry or thirsty or a stranger or needing clothes or sick or in prison, and did not help you?'

'He will reply, 'Truly I tell you, whatever you did not do for one of the least of these, you did not do for me.'

'Then they will go away to eternal punishment, but the righteous to eternal life.'"

Dad understood this command and strove to help people. He wanted to help those that were less fortunate than he was in this world. He worked at homeless shelters everywhere he lived: central Illinois, northern Illinois, and southern Florida. He donated countless hours to various churches to ensure that they were accomplishing their goal of reaching the lost for the Lord. Although he would hate to hear it, for many people, Bruce exemplified the saintly life.

How about you? Dad wrote the following commentary back in the 1990's, but the message still applies: What are you doing to help those less fortunate?

Two Men Cared (Bruce)

Acts 3:1-8 (NIV)

"One day Peter and John were going up to the temple at the time of prayer-at three in the afternoon. Now a man crippled from birth was being carried to the temple gate called Beautiful, where he was put every day to beg from those going into the temple courts. When he saw Peter and John about to enter, he asked them for money. Peter looked straight at him, as did John. Then Peter said, "Look at us!" So the man gave them his attention, expecting to get something from them. Then Peter said, "Silver or gold I do not have, but what I have I give you. In the name of Jesus Christ of Nazareth, walk." Taking him by the right hand, he helped

him up, and instantly the man's feet and ankles became strong. He jumped to his feet and began to walk. Then he went with them into the temple courts, walking and jumping, and praising God."

(Spoken by the beggar from Acts 3:1-8)

I heard them coming,
    just like all the others.
And I said, friend,
    don't overlook my begging.
T'was nature that dealt me this pain.
    Forsaken now am I,
Cursed, laughed at and ridiculed.
    There is nothing left in life to gain.

Just give me a couple of mites,
    and then you can be on your way.
I'll be alright you see,
    for I have lived like this many a day.
But mites they would not give.
    And instead they answered with a harsh voice,
"Rise up, you're no longer lame,
    walk away and give to the Lord your rejoice".

Now these two men who cared,
    saw my needs, and gave me more.
Took my fears, so I'm no longer scared,
    and gave me hope in the name of the Lord.
To others I must now go and teach,
    and spread the word for others to know,
That in Jesus we can all reach,
    the promise of tomorrow and eternity.

Do we really care about others in need or do we tend to take the easy way? Isn't it easier sometimes just to give money and walk away? True, we must first meet physical needs of others, but what about emotional or spiritual needs? The *latter two, requires a giving of ourselves for others while the giving of money, although at times important, allows us to remain detached and uninvolved. Each of us are what we are today because of other's concerns for us or the lack thereof. Will we be remembered as someone who cared?*

Bruce W. VanderKolk
21 October 1994

October 2, 2015 (Bruce)

Had my third treatment on Sept 29, 2015, at 09:30am. Was done by 11:15am. Treatment went ok and I made the two hours. However, after an hour and when I was back at the hotel, started having abdomen pain which became severe, bladder spasms, and diarrhea. This went on for 7-8 hours before it started to subside. Not a very pleasant afternoon and evening.

My CT scan was normal which was good news.

October 31, 2015

Had my last treatment on Oct 20, 2015 (total six treatments). Still bad after-effects and seemed to last almost two days this time. Seems like it takes a little longer to get over the treatments each time. Pray that the treatments will have been effective. Saw the doctor on the 22nd of Oct: there is now the treatment present in the local medical facility so if I go on maintenance every three months I can get the treatment there.

December 2, 2015

Today I saw the doctor and had another scope. There was no sign of a tumor and the inside of the bladder looked the best it has since the first diagnosis in November, 2014. There were two small red spots but the doctor was not too concerned and indicated it could be from the surgery/treatment or a small residue of the cancer. The doctor has scheduled me for another scope in March, 2016. If that scope shows a good result, then the doctor mentioned about me going on treatment maintenance. This would be three treatments every three months. If results continue to be good then the treatments would go out to 6 months and this would continue for three years. This is going to be a very long process. If in three months there is a questionable area then it is back to another biopsy. We did not discuss what would happen if it was positive.

I consider this to be good news and thank God for the results. I do not have any spasms and the urge to urinate is not there. It is like the good old days. God has given me more time; I just hope I can use the time to honor Him.

2016

Uncertainty (Roger)

We were fortunate to be able to spend the holidays together and watch the calendar change from 2015 to 2016. We spent the holidays at my brother's house in northern Illinois, creating memories, laughing, and enjoying each other's company. One special memory was watching Riley, my brother's dog, crazily attack the snow when the snowblower was removing snow from the driveway. The dog just couldn't quite understand why he wasn't able to clamp his teeth on this white powder that was being shot out from a strange machine.

Our family has never placed a high degree of importance on celebrating the coming of the new year on New Year's Eve. But we certainly were ready to move on from all of the challenges that 2015 presented, especially to Dad's health. We all were looking forward to the possibility of moving past bladder cancer in the new year.

But of course life doesn't always go as planned.

We don't have a journal entry from Dad until March of this year so it is impossible to know his exact emotional state in early 2016. But it is reasonable to believe that going through one medical issue after another since 2009 had left him frustrated with the status of his journey. For 7 years, he trusted that God had a plan for his struggle and would be with Dad until the end of this life.

It's easy to trust when we can see the end. It's difficult to trust when you can't see the end, which is where Dad was going into 2016.

One of the most powerful verses in the Bible can be found in Proverbs 3:5-6: "Trust in the Lord with all your heart and lean not on your own understanding; in all your ways submit to him, and he will make your paths straight." (NIV)

This verse likely encapsulated Dad's emotional and spiritual state as the calendar turned to a new year: He was trusting God. But, as you will read, his trust continued to be stretched.

I Had To See (Bruce)

I had to see for myself,
Though I was considered to be an outcast.
So I followed behind,
Trying not to be noticed.
Who was this tall man,
That seemed to speak in riddles
And showed no partiality.
A man who said the time has come
As so many listen intently.
I followed Him to Galilee,
And unto Capernaum.
He said He must preach the good news,
Not just to us but to other towns.
I watched Him at Lake of Gennesaret,
And as He walked through the grainfields.
Like a magnet He drew crowds from
Judea, Jerusalem, Tyre and Sidon.
What a strange message He had,
About a reward in Heaven and turning
The other cheek. This was certainly not
The way of the Romans and what
The leaders wanted to hear.
The more I heard, the more I
Became mesmerized by the message.
It was a message of love and hope,
Of forgiveness and faith.
As I followed Him from town to town
And heard Him claim the good news,
I too gave my life to Him.

Bruce VanderKolk
February 17, 2016

March 9, 2016 (Bruce)

Had the scope today. Not the best of news as the doctor wants to biopsy the two areas that were noticed back in December. Doesn't appear that there are any new growths and these may not be as red as they were in December.

Nevertheless it is still like being punched. This has been going on nearly 1 ½ years since I was first diagnosed with the bladder cancer. I am not sure if we are any nearer to eliminating the cancer. It is hard to keep up a "good front" like everything is fine. At times it is hard to get motivated to do anything. Sleep works good as you no longer think about it.

It is also hard not to be constantly thinking about the cancer and the future. I suspect only people who have gone through cancer can relate to these feelings. Others cannot but they do their best or they appear not to want to talk about it. Maybe they think the cancer will spread to them if they ask questions and talk about it with you.

Recently we had a Bible class study on a video series by Craig Groeschel on "When God seems Uncooperative." Sometimes when we pray it does not seem like God hears our prayers. The Bible provides the following truths about prayer:

1. True prayer isn't about getting our way, but surrendering our will to God. (2 Cor 12:7)
2. Prayer reminds us that we're not in control and keeps us close to the One who is. (2 Cor 12:8&9)
3. Prayer isn't just asking, but trusting. (2 Cor 12:9-10)

Your mind may understand these three points but your heart and emotions do not. I need to pray that my entire being becomes able to accept these points.

March 25, 2016

Well, you never know. My three biopsies were all negative. I must have little faith as I just knew they would be positive. You ask for prayers and when they are answered, you are surprised. What is wrong with that picture? Craig Groeschel was right. It is hard to describe the emotions that I am going through now. I should be flying high but I am not; nor am I down. I guess you could *describe it as being in a state of shock. You build yourself up to accept the negative and when it does not happen it is hard to deal with the positive.*

I will now start a maintenance program of three weeks of treatment in May followed by another scope in June. The doctor said I did not need to do the treatment, however, without the treatments my odds of the cancer coming back is 40% and with the treatment it drops to 25%. This will be a long process and hopefully we will be able to move to treatments every six months.

Why Worry (Roger)

"I must have little faith as I just knew they would be positive."

Imagine sitting and waiting for a phone call from the doctor that will radically effect your life. That had to be a time of constant thinking about the possible outcomes of the test. Worrying about whether it was bad news.

Many of you reading this book don't have to imagine this scenario: You're living it.

After reading about Bruce's faith in Book 1 and in this book thus far, there is very little evidence to suggest that Dad had little faith. Quite the opposite actually: His faith was strong, deep to his core. He had spent his entire adult life actively studying and growing in his faith and at this point had a faith stronger than most of us.

The more likely picture of Dad's emotional state was that he was letting worry get the best of him. Which is perfectly understandable with all of the storms that life had thrown his way. The journal date on the previous entry was March 25th, 2016, nearly two years after he started his fight with bladder cancer. As his journal reflects, there were numerous days where the bad news outweighed the good news; it is natural that his mindset was worried about these last round of tests.

As Christians, we are encouraged not to worry. Actually, we are not just encouraged, we are commanded not to worry. Despite his circumstances, Dad should have read the following Bible verses that day to see what Jesus had to say about worry:

Matthew 6:25-34 (NIV):

"Therefore I tell you, do not worry about your life, what you will eat or drink; or about your body, what you will wear. Is not life more than food, and the body more than clothes? Look at the birds of the air; they do not sow or reap or store away in barns, and yet your heavenly Father feeds them. Are you not much more valuable than they? Can any one of you by worrying add a single hour to your life?

'And why do you worry about clothes? See how the flowers of the field grow. They do not labor or spin. Yet I tell you that not even Solomon in all his splendor was dressed like one of these. If that is how God clothes the grass of the field, which is here today and tomorrow is thrown into the fire, will he not much more clothe you—you of little faith? So do not worry, saying, 'What shall we eat?' or 'What shall we drink?' or 'What shall we wear?' For the pagans run after all these things, and your heavenly Father knows that you need them. But seek first his kingdom and his righteousness, and all these things will be given to you as well. Therefore do not worry about tomorrow, for tomorrow will worry about itself. Each day has enough trouble of its own.'"

Worry is bad. If you read between the lines in the passage above, the conclusion could be drawn that Jesus was upset that some of His followers were experiencing worry. It's almost as if He took it personally and was taking them behind the woodshed for a chat.

Worry:

1. **Paralyzes your present** - There is nothing like worry that completely and utterly manifests itself in your mind. Worry is all consuming once it gains a foothold in your thoughts. Sure, it starts small with a quick thought: Why hasn't the doctor called me back after the test? Then, like a snowball that turns into an avalanche, your thoughts are filled with thoughts such as "It must be bad news otherwise the doctor's nurse would have called me. It must be very bad because the doctor hasn't called because they want me to come into the office where they can deliver the news personally. Will I need surgery?" Etc. Once the avalanche starts, it's not too long until

it's all you can think about. Your relationships suffer because the worry makes you only think about yourself. Your job suffers. Your family suffers. Your health suffers. With all of his tests, Dad's present was definitely paralyzed whenever he let worry gain too much of a foothold in his thoughts.

2. **Threatens your future** - When we worry too much about the present, worry then starts to entangle itself in our future because we worry about the wrong things. Instead of thinking about things that we can control, we worry about things outside of our control. We then make plans for the future accordingly. In other words, our plans for the future are modified based on a faulty foundation (worry) rather than a firm foundation. If you're fighting an illness, your future will definitely be impacted. But rather than adjusting for something that is actually happening, or something that could possibly happen, worry causes us to create bad plans for the future. We cancel the upcoming family gathering because we think we won't feel good enough to travel. There were a few examples in the previous book as to how some of Dad's future plans were impacted because he was worried about how his health struggles would affect him.

3. **Usurps God's authority** - Worry is selfishness. Worry makes us focus on ourselves. Re-read the two above bullets. Notice how many times worry is focused on ourselves rather than on other people. Worry says we want to solve the problem ourselves. No, that's not entirely accurate: Worry says we *need* to solve the problem ourselves. When we decide that we need to solve the problems ourselves, we lessen, if not completely remove, God's impact and power on the situation. In essence, we are playing God. We think we are powerful enough to fix the situation instead of relying on the One who created the universe. This is one of the aspects of worry that bothered Dad: deep down he realized that God was in control of the impact of the bladder cancer on his body. He believed that healing would come from God and God alone and that worrying about each and every test result would do nothing to eliminate the cancer. Dad didn't want his own fear to impact his relationship with his heavenly Father.

4. **Minimizes your Faith** - The Bible tells us that faith is "the substance of things hoped for, the evidence of things not seen" (Hebrews 11:1, KJV). When we place our faith in God, we enter into a relationship where we acknowledge that God is all powerful and has a plan for our lives. Hebrews chapter 11 is filled with examples of people in the Bible that placed their faith in God. All of us are in a similar position: Will our lives turn out like we want? It's possible. But we must have faith that when we enter into a relationship with God, our plan is to align with a plan to serve Him as effectively as possible. We are all unique and are called for different purposes. Your situation and struggle is different than Dad's. But through faith, you can serve God daily just like Dad. Build up those around you. Serve the weak and downtrodden. Focus on being a light to others despite your struggles.

5. **Weakens your witness** - The result of all of the above aspects of worry is that when we let worry control our lives, we are no different than those without faith.

Easier said than done of course. But isn't that what this life is all about? Improving ourselves so that our tomorrow is better than today? Lessening worry is possible; Dad provided numerous examples throughout his struggle. One time in particular is at the exact time frame that Dad wrote this journal entry. What's interesting about the entry is what Dad didn't record: I was visiting Mom and Dad in Southwest Florida from March 25th to April 3rd. During this visit I remember going to the beach, dining in local restaurants, engaging in other tourist activities, and attending church with them. Throughout this entire visit Dad didn't shrink from spending time together by being wrapped up in fear over the next potential phone call. He didn't let worry determine his life.

Going cold turkey and eliminating worry totally overnight simply isn't going to happen for the vast majority of us. If you're fighting an illness, there are a myriad of tests, procedures, and similar circumstances that bring concern today, tomorrow, and the next day.

But. You can start today. Choose something small. Decrease your "worry bucket" by giving it over to God in prayer. See how He answers your prayer.

Then tomorrow, choose another small thing. And another. See how God works in your life by decreasing your worries.

May 7, 2016 (Bruce)

Had my first maintenance treatment yesterday at 7:15 am. Really do not like these treatments - the rest of the day was not fun. Feeling better today. Two more treatments.

May 21, 2016

Well, I had my third treatment yesterday. I do not think the side-effects were as bad as the previous treatments, although they still were not pleasant. Today I even ventured out which I had not done previously. Now we wait until June 10, 2016, for another scope to see how effective the treatments have been and if there is any cancer present.

June 10, 2016

Saw the doctor this morning at 7:10 am and had another Cystoscopy. If I was to describe the results in terms of a weather forecast, it would be today is not going to be sunny but there will also be no thunderstorms. The day will be cloudy.

The results showed some redness in the same area as the last biopsy (which was negative) but no signs of a tumor. However, the redness could be irritation or the beginning of a cancer tumor. The doctor is going to send out the urine sample to see if there are any cancer cells and then wants to do another Cystoscopy on September 23, 2016. If they do find cancer cells then another biopsy will be done as we understand. If there are no cancer cells, and the next Cystoscopy is ok, I will probably have another round of three maintenance treatments.

The cloud over my head and the uncertainty of the future continues to be present. It has now been 1 ½ years since the cancer was diagnosed.

Simply Pray (Roger)

Growing up, the VanderKolk boys were taught to pray. We prayed before bedtime. We prayed for meals before we ate, whether at home or at restaurants. We prayed in church. And we were encouraged to pray on our own. Prayer is a very important component of our lives.

Why did we pray so often while growing up? Why was it important for Dad and Mom to ensure that their sons developed a prayer habit? Quite simply it was because the Bible said to pray many times and even provided examples of how we should pray. Prayer is such an important part of the Bible that it is mentioned in one form or another over 350 times! The following is just a glimpse of the many exhortations to pray in the Bible that Dad and Mom used as their foundation:

- "Pray for those who persecute you." (Matthew 5:44, NIV)
- "Pray continually." (1 Thessalonians 5:17, NIV)
- "Do not be anxious about anything, but in every situation, by prayer and petition, with thanksgiving, present your requests to God." (Philippians 4:6, NIV)
- "Is anyone among you in trouble? Let them pray." (James 5:13, NIV)
- "Answer me when I call to you, my righteous God. Give me relief from my distress; have mercy on me and hear my prayer." (Psalms 4:1, NIV)
- "Now when Daniel learned that the decree had been published, he went home to his upstairs room where the windows opened toward Jerusalem. Three times a day he got down on his knees and prayed, giving thanks to his God, just as he had done before." (Daniel 6:10, NIV)

In spite of all the various commands in the Bible that we are given to pray, many of our prayers are simplistic in nature. Why do we pray? Because we want or need something.

In college, I was privileged to form friendships with a bunch of God-fearing men. We were given the affectionate nickname of "Bowser's Idiot Friends" after some of our antics while supporting the soccer team. We took this name in pride and shortened it to "BIF". As the name implies, we weren't the sharpest crayons when it came to our devotion to the world's most famous sport. We traveled to away games and tailgated before games, riling the opposing fans. When we found the bleachers of our school lacking, we carried couches to the home games! Evenings after dinner we could be found playing soccer between apartment buildings. We even took the sport of soccer for physical education credit.

But more importantly, we were intensely devoted to our faith. We created a weekly prayer group to seek God's guidance and assistance with events in our lives. The prayer meetings were of total transparency (no "unspokens"): If someone had a request, it was presented to the group. After all the requests were presented, each member of the group selected items to add to their individual prayer list. Then they would pray for those requests during the meeting and also throughout the week. One of the rules was that you weren't able to pray for yourself because that was assumed to be happening outside of the meeting. We were privileged to witness God blessing our prayers and experienced many good works in our lives and in the lives of our families and friends. Ours was a collective prayer habit: others before ourselves.

Today, I find myself with the same mentality: others before myself. There are plenty of serious, big issues that my friends and acquaintances are going through. These issues are significantly greater than my own condition. Thus, more times than not, when I pray, I'm praying for someone else before myself. But this probably isn't the right way to pray either.

So what is the right way to pray?

Thankfully, Jesus gave us a prayer blueprint in Matthew 6:5-14. If you've spent even a little time in church, you've heard of the common name for this prayer example: The Lord's Prayer. Would it surprise you to know that a simple blueprint is found in this passage, providing points of how we should pray? We simply have to learn the "ACTS" of prayer.

Adoration:
- "Our Father in heaven, hallowed be your name. Your kingdom come, your will be done, on earth as it is in heaven."
- Throughout the Bible we are reminded that one of our purposes on earth is to worship the Creator of the universe. When we acknowledge God for who He is, it sets the framework as we seek to enter into God's presence through

prayer. Acknowledging that God is God sets our mindset because it reminds us that we are not God.

- Biblical Example: When Jesus separated himself from the disciples to pray before the crucifixion, his first words in his prayer were "My Father." (Matthew 26:39, NIV)

Confession:

- "And forgive us our debts, as we also have forgiven our debtors."
- Each step in the prayer blueprint that Jesus provided physically puts us a little bit lower in a physical stature. First we bow out of reverence to God and who He is. Then we put ourselves a little lower as we acknowledge just how far off we are from His holiness because of our sin.
- Confession also helps to clear our conscience because God has promised to remove our sin when we confess to Him.
- Biblical Example: "If we confess our sins, He is faithful and just and will forgive us our sins and purify us from all unrighteousness." (1 John 1:9, NIV)

Thanksgiving:

- "Give us today our daily bread."
- After we have realized that we are very far off from God and His holiness, this next step is a natural response to God's grace and mercy. It is important to realize that this step is not thanksgiving for what God will do because we pray (aka: "Thanks for letting me win the lottery") but is instead thanksgiving that God is all powerful and is able to provide our needs.
- The phrase itself doesn't look like one of thanksgiving; it sounds instead like a precursor to supplication. What's interesting is that many of the translations of the Bible use the exact two words in this verse as the NIV translation: "daily bread". The implication behind this phrase is that God provides for us what we need ("daily bread") and we are to be thankful for His provisions.
- Biblical Example: "Do not be anxious about anything, but in

every situation, by prayer and petition, with thanksgiving, present your requests to God." (Philippians 4:6, NIV)

Supplication:
- "And lead us not into temptation, but deliver us from the evil one."
- Finally, after we have acknowledged God for who He is, after confessing that we are woefully short of His holiness, and after thanking Him for His grace and mercy in our lives, we are able to present our requests to God. There is no prescribed manner through which to present our requests to the Creator of the universe, but we should take care to not make this a simple grocery list. We need to reflect on the outcome of what we are asking from God and how He is able to fulfill those requests.
- Biblical Example: The above verse also applies to this aspect of prayer as well. "Do not be anxious about anything, but in every situation, by prayer and petition, with thanksgiving, present your requests to God." (Philippians 4:6, NIV)

There is little doubt that Dad prayed often: his journal is littered with references to prayer. Dad studied the Bible enough that he would have followed the above blueprint.

What's your method? Do you have time for adoration? For confession? For thanksgiving? For supplication? If you don't have a trusted method, I encourage you to consider the above method.

July 29, 2016 (Bruce)

Well, this was a kick in the butt day. Around noon I received a call from the doctor that my urine sample was positive for cancer cells. The doctor wants to schedule surgery as soon as possible to scrape the red area in the bladder. After that it will be more treatments but at this time the doctor is not sure what. May be the usual treatment or a combination of it and something else. Need to wait until after the surgery. We are going to try to go to Florida after Vanessa's (niece) wedding.

August 22, 2016

Well today is the day for the third bladder cancer surgery. Need to be at the medical facility at 1:45 pm, so surgery probably will not be until 3-3:30 pm assuming the doctor is not running behind. Visiting nurse comes in starting tonight.

August 25, 2016

It is three days since my surgery and I am finally feeling well enough to write a brief summary. The surgery was at around 3:30 pm. I am guessing I was in recovery around 4:30, at least when I woke up. After a while I was taken back to a room and Donna was able to join me. It wasn't until about 7:15 that the doctor came in. There was a major surgery after mine which delayed the doctor. The news was not that good. The doctor found new areas, which were removed, plus one was near the entrance to the drain from one of the kidneys. Not what we wanted to hear. I really was expecting better news. The doctor wanted to do a CT scan of my kidneys and to start the treatments again for six weeks. If this doesn't work I do not know what will happen next or what will happen if the cancer is found in the kidneys.

Right now it is hard (very difficult) to be upbeat about my situation.

Recovery has been slow. As usual it is hard to kick start the bowel movement so I took some medicine. It worked but now I am having some after-effects such as cramps, gas, diarrhea, etc. I did get the catheter out on the 24th which was very much welcomed. I have a visiting nurse who comes in and checks on me. The nurse was here the night of my surgery. Monday next week should be the last if everything is ok.

I have received some cards already and best wishes by phone and text. As some of the cards or texts had a scripture, I thought it would be good to type them out and read them over. The words are as follows:

Psalm 59:16 New International Version (NIV):
    "But I will sing of your strength
    In the morning I will sing of your love;
    For you are my fortress,
    My refuge in times of trouble"
    (Card from Mary Cheetwood, Oregon Church of God, on August 24, 2016)

Lamentations 3:22-23 New International Version (NIV):
"Because of Lord's great love we are not consumed,
For his compassions never fail.
They are new every morning;
Great is your faithfulness"
(Card received from Jack and Phyllis Wyatt on August 24, 2016)

Isaiah 41:10 New International Version (NIV):
"So do not fear, for I am with you; Do not be dismayed, for I am your God. I will strengthen you and help you; I will uphold you with my righteous right hand."
(Mary Lou Aulbert, text to Donna on August 23, 2016)

Luke 9:11 New International Version (NIV):
"But the crowds learned about it and followed him. He welcomed them and spoke to them about the kingdom of God, and healed those who needed healing."
(Card received from Merle and Lois Lash on August 24, 2016. Also on the back was an paragraph from an article in the "Guideposts Magazine" in 2016 titled "Wishes with Wings". This really spoke to me and reinforced that God is with me during this trial.)

Psalm 29:11 New International Version (NIV)
"The Lord gives strength to his people; the Lord blesses his people with peace."
(Card received from Harold and Juanita Moore on August 24, 2016. Also received this exact verse on a card that I received from Anchor Christian Church on August 29, 2016. The Lord works in mysterious ways!)

Isaiah 40:8 New King James Version (NKJV)
"The grass withers, the flower fades, but the word of our God stands forever."
(Card received from Linda and Michael Hoffman on August 27, 2016. Michael is the Pastor at the church we attend in Oregon. Also on the back of the card was a clip from a "Guideposts Magazine" article from 2015 titled "Life is Like a Garden".)

Romans 1:9-10 New Century Version (NCV)
"God...knows that I always mention you every time I pray."

(Card received from Merle and Lois Lash on September 10, 2016. Also on the back of the card was another clip from "Guideposts Magazine" titled "Dialing with Your Heart". This was written by Van Varner in an 2016 edition of the magazine.)

I have received countless other cards from friends and family, too numerous to include in this journal.

Encouragement (Roger)

The preceding journal entry ended with a snapshot of the encouragement cards that Dad received from his friends and family. He was really touched that someone would take a break from their busy schedule and take a few minutes to personalize a card with the intent to boost his spirits. He was full of gratitude: he kept every card and made an attempt to personally thank everyone who sent him a card while he was dealing with his struggles.

Encouragement is so important that the word itself is found over 30 times in the Bible. Thirty instances in the Bible we are encouraged to be people of encouragement for others. There is even a person in the Bible with a name that literally means "Son of Encouragement". That person was Barnabas who was first introduced early in the book of Acts:

"Joseph, a Levite from Cyprus, whom the apostles called Barnabas (which means 'son of encouragement') sold a field he owned and brought the money and put it at the apostles' feet." (Acts 4:36-37, NIV)

From this lowly introduction, Barnabas would go on to travel the world, proclaiming the gospel with the apostle Paul. Barnabas was a key contributor to the spread of Christianity.

How cool would it be to be known as a "son or daughter of encouragement"? Or, to be quite pointed, what is stopping us from taking time to reach out to a friend, a family member, or an acquaintance with an act of encouragement? Are we really too busy to do one of the following?

- **Greeting Card physically sent through the mail:** Purchase a card and stamp. Write the message of encouragement in the card. Lick the flaps and seal the envelope. Address the card. Affix a stamp. Drop the card in the mailbox.
- **Email:** Turn on computer. Open email program. Find email address of intended recipient. Write subject line. Type message of encouragement. Click Send.
- **Text:** Find person's name and phone number in list of contacts. Type message of encouragement. Click send.
- **Phone call:** Find person's name and phone number in list of contacts. Push Call. Verbally deliver message of encouragement. Listen if they want to talk. Hang up.

All of these are easy and low cost methods of communicating encouragement to someone who is going through a hard time. Five minutes and less than $10. This seems like a high return on investment (ROI) in terms of impact on the other person.

We can also offer encouragement to those not necessarily going through a life-or-death struggle. We interact with people everyday and can share encouragement with them as well. We can tell a co-worker "I really like how you handled that difficult colleague". We could tell the store worker "good job" when they do something to improve our shopping experience. We can thank a public servant such as a firefighter or police officer.

We may never hear back from that person but that's really not the point: It is not about us, it is about trying to make their day brighter.

But to be completely transparent, it is not all about them. There is also a component of reaching out to others with encouragement that assists us in our battle. The act of delivering encouragement also distracts us from our battle and struggle. When we concentrate our efforts on doing things that improve the lives of others, we focus on ourselves less.

The question for us then is: How do we become known as a "son of encouragement" or a "daughter of encouragement"? What can you do today to provide encouragement to a friend, a family member, a co-worker, or an acquaintance?

September 10, 2016 (Bruce)

Well, this has not been a pleasant week. Last Saturday night after dinner I started to develop a pain in my lower right abdomen. This continued and got more severe-very sharp pain. I could not lie in bed so I sat in my recliner. Then about 2:15 am the pain got better - never went away totally. I was able to go to bed and get some sleep.

As Monday was Labor Day I could not go to the doctor even though the pain was still present. However, it was not sufficient to warrant a trip to the ER.

On Tues. morning I called my primary care doctor and had an appointment in the afternoon. The doctor thought it might be diverticulitis and put me on two antibiotics. As of now I am still bothered by a dull pain.

To cap it off, on September 8 in the morning after waking up I passed very large blood clots in the urine, about size of dime or larger. As it continued on the 9th, I called my surgeon. The doctor thought it might be old clots in part because my urine was clear afterwards and during the day. I am to see the doctor next week and also to find out results of CT scan of the kidneys and urinary tract I had on Thursday.

My request is simple; I just want to feel better.

Gray Days (Roger)

"My request is simple; I just want to feel better."

Sometimes encouragement isn't enough to make a difference in the emotional wellbeing of those we love as they navigate their journey through difficult circumstances. Sometimes they are experiencing a day when life loses all of its color, all of its beauty, and all of its joy. The day is simply gray. No matter what they do, no matter what we do, their thoughts are negative. They are in a funk that they just can't seem to escape. They are depressed.

Dad was human: much of what he did during his struggle was really good; he laid the framework for thriving amidst life-threatening diseases. But he wasn't perfect; he missed things and made mistakes during his struggle. One of those was handling depression. At no point during his multi-year struggle with various types of cancers and other diseases did he seek help to learn how to navigate through periods of depression.

Like Dad, despite all of our best intentions, we all face periods of depression. Objectively, Dad knew that he was depressed and deep down he knew what he could do to weather the storms during the gray days. He knew the following would be helpful during his struggle:

- **Acknowledge it** - Our society continues to look down on depression as if it is not a real illness. We must confront the stigma our society has placed on depression and provide compassion for those suffering from it.

- **Share** - Find close friends and family members that will walk with you during the periods of depression. Too often we are close-minded and internalize our thoughts as we navigate through those periods. Dad didn't go down this path; he was old schooled, stoic, and bottled up his feelings. Dad could have been helped had he embrace Proverbs 12:25: "Anxiety weighs down the heart, but a kind word cheers it up" (NIV). Perhaps this is too simplistic, but there is a reason this exhortation is found in the Bible: it's truth.

- **Realize that it is only Temporary** - The wording throughout this section is specific: We encounter *periods* of depression. Sunshine will return.

- **Seek Help** - Whether from a professional, a support group, or friends / relatives that have battled depression, seek their wisdom. Learn from their experience. Read the Bible. The Bible is full of people that battled depression: Moses, Elijah, David (book of Psalms), Job, Jonah, and even the Apostle Paul. Meditate on their words and learn from their approach to God during periods of depression.

- **Be Still** - Disconnect from today's technological life: turn off the television, the computer, the cell phone. Spend time alone, in quietness, with God. Seek His power; use these times to dwell upon Him to strengthen your faith. Reflect on the simplicity and majesty of Psalms 46:10: "Be still, and know that I am God" (NIV).

- **Dispense Grace & Mercy** - Of the countless memes in our culture today, perhaps the strongest ones are those that encourage us not to judge other people because we don't know the battle they are facing. This is relevant when we go through times of depression. When we are depressed, when we are living in a world of gray, we are not ourselves and our actions are such that we need grace and mercy from other people. We also need to apply that grace and mercy to others when they are struggling internally with depression.

Periods of depression are a consequence of the fall of man and the curse from the original sin. The periods seem to last forever, with no clear path towards resolution. But, there is reason to have hope because you are not alone. Because He was fully human, it is reasonable to believe that Jesus went through periods of depression. We read about one such time in Matthew 26:

- Verses 36-38: "Then Jesus went with his disciples to a place called Gethsemane, and he said to them, 'Sit here while I go over there and pray.' He took Peter and the two sons of Zebedee along with him, and he began to be sorrowful and troubled. Then he said to them, 'My soul is overwhelmed with sorrow to the point of death. Stay here and keep watch with me.'" (NIV)
- Verse 39: "Going a little farther, he fell with his face to the ground and prayed, 'My Father, if it is possible, may this cup be taken from me. Yet not as I will, but as you will.'" (NIV)

Dad wrote the following nearly two decades prior to his diagnosis with prostate cancer. The message of this writing is relevant to his struggle with depression then and is relevant to our struggles today. Try as we might, often times we will be unsuccessful in avoiding periods of depression. But when those periods come, we have hope. We can take refuge in God's promise to always be with us.

The Tree of Life (Bruce)

Revelation 2:7 - "To the one who is victorious, I will give the right to eat from the tree of life, which is in the paradise of God." (NIV)

The path to the paradise of God and the fruit of the tree of life is available to all who call upon the name of our Lord Jesus Christ. This assurance has been made possible by the death of our Lord upon the cross. As I reflected upon the cross, I visually traveled the life of our Lord, from the prophetic announcement, to His birth, His life, His suffering and death upon the cross to His ultimate victory over death.

As I pondered upon the journey of our Lord, I saw His strength and majesty. I thought of the cross and saw within the structure of the cross the end of another life. I saw a parallel in the life of the wood which formed the cross and the life of our Savior who eventually hung upon the cross. I attempted to capture the similarity of the two and called the analogy "The Tree of Life". Just as the tree must die in order to be made into a cross, our Lord and Savior died to form a cross: a cross which provides for mankind the bridge to the paradise of God.

The Tree of Life

I floated to earth as a seed.
> *In fertile soil I grew to be.*
> *In quiet splendor I burst forth,*
> *With dignity and majesty.*

Seeing the ray of sparkling light,
> *Several stood in awe at my sight.*
> *Though young and tender I was now,*
> *Many marveled with joy delight.*

My roots grew strong and shallow not,
> *Forming the anchor of my lot.*
> *Strong and sturdy I would become,*
> *A beacon ne'er to be forgot.*

Over the years my branches grew,
    Providing hope and strength anew.
    With age my time was coming soon,
    For I must help more than these few.

I saw them gather carefully,
    With eyes of steel and trickery.
    Through scorns and sneering I stood firm,
    Yielding not to their mockery.

They won the battle for my life.
    And had me taken to the site.
    Upon the hill I gave my all,
    Forming the cross for those who call.

Bruce W. VanderKolk (7 December 1997)

September 30, 2016 (Bruce)

Well I had my first treatment of six this morning. It was not a pleasant experience and for 12 hours it was not fun. I can see why some people after so many treatments say "no more". However, I suspect that others may even have a harder time after cancer treatments.

A couple of days ago a long time friend gave me a small booklet that he and his wife had read. There were a few meaningful verses from the Bible within the book, which I have added to my list. I have been keeping a list of Bible verses that have spoken to, provided comfort for, and encouraged me for the past few years. Outside of the verses I've already included, I have decided to include a partial list of these verses and their application to me in this journal. The list, in order as they are found in the Bible is as follows:

Old Testament Encouragement:

1.   **Keep God's commands**: *"He said, 'If you listen carefully to the Lord your God and do what is right in his eyes, if you pay attention to his commands and keep all his decrees, I will not bring on you any of the diseases I brought on the Egyptians, for I am the Lord, who heals you.'"* (*Exodus 15:26, NIV*)

2. ***Worship God:*** *"Worship the Lord your God, and his blessing will be on your food and water. I will take away sickness from among you." (Exodus 23:25, NIV)*

3. ***God protects those who love Him in this life and the next:*** *"The Lord will keep you free from every disease. He will not inflict on you the horrible diseases you knew in Egypt, but he will inflict them on all who hate you." (Deuteronomy 7:15, NIV)*

4. ***God has made His will known to us and we would do well to follow it****: "This day I call the heavens and the earth as witnesses against you that I have set before you life and death, blessings and curses. Now choose life, so that you and your children may live." (Deuteronomy 30:19, NIV)*

5. ***The importance of meditating on God's Word:*** *"Keep this Book of the Law always on your lips; meditate on it day and night, so that you may be careful to do everything written in it. Then you will be prosperous and successful." (Joshua 1:8, NIV)*

6. ***God's Plan is complete:*** *"Not one of all the Lord's good promises to Israel failed; every one was fulfilled" (Joshua 21:45, NIV)*

7. ***Serve God. Always****: "But if serving the Lord seems undesirable to you, then choose for yourselves this day whom you will serve, whether the gods your ancestors served beyond the Euphrates, or the gods of the Amorites, in whose land you are living. But as for me and my household, we will serve the Lord." (Joshua 24:15, NIV)*

8. ***God heals:*** *"Blessed is the one whom God corrects; so do not despise the discipline of the Almighty. For he wounds, but he also binds up; he injures, but his hands also heal." (Job 4:17-18, NIV)*

9. ***God can do all things and we would do well to believe Him****: "Then Job replied to the Lord: 'I know that you can do all things; no purpose of yours can be thwarted. You asked, 'Who is this that obscures my plans without knowledge?' Surely I spoke of things I did not understand, things too wonderful for me to know. You said, 'Listen now, and I will speak; I will question you, and you shall answer me.' My ears had heard of you but now my eyes have seen you. Therefore I despise myself and repent in dust and ashes.'" (Job 42:1-6, NIV)*

10. ***God is with us. Always:*** *"The Lord is my shepherd, I lack nothing. He makes me lie down in green pastures, he leads me beside quiet waters, he refreshes my soul. He guides me along the right paths for his name's sake. Even though I walk through the darkest valley, I will fear no evil,*

for you are with me; your rod and your staff, they comfort me. You prepare a table before me in the presence of my enemies. You anoint my head with oil; my cup overflows. Surely your goodness and love will follow me all the days of my life, and I will dwell in the house of the Lord forever." (Psalms 23:1-6, NIV)

11. **God knows when we need to be rescued and will deliver us***: "'Because he loves me,' says the Lord, 'I will rescue him; I will protect him, for he acknowledges my name. He will call on me, and I will answer him; I will be with him in trouble, I will deliver him and honor him. With long life I will satisfy him and show him my salvation.'" (Psalm 91:14-16, NIV)*

12. **God is worthy of our praise regardless whether or not He delivers us from our struggles:** *"Praise the Lord, my soul; all my inmost being, praise his holy name. Praise the Lord, my soul, and forget not all his benefits— who forgives all your sins and heals all your diseases, who redeems your life from the pit and crowns you with love and compassion, who satisfies your desires with good things so that your youth is renewed like the eagle's." (Psalm 103:1-5, NIV)*

13. **God rescues and heals***: "He sent out his word and healed them; he rescued them from the grave." (Psalm 107:20, NIV)*

14. **Deliverance and salvation are found through God:** *"I was pushed back and about to fall, but the Lord helped me. The Lord is my strength and my defense; he has become my salvation. Shouts of joy and victory resound in the tents of the righteous: 'The Lord's right hand has done mighty things! The Lord's right hand is lifted high; the Lord's right hand has done mighty things!' I will not die but live, and will proclaim what the Lord has done. The Lord has chastened me severely, but he has not given me over to death. Open for me the gates of the righteous; I will enter and give thanks to the Lord. This is the gate of the Lord through which the righteous may enter. I will give you thanks, for you answered me; you have become my salvation." (Psalms 118:14-21, NIV)*

15. **God is good. Forever, He is good***: "Give thanks to the Lord, for he is good; his love endures forever (Psalms 118:29, NIV)*

16. **God's Word (The Bible) is a powerful repository of instruction and advice for life:** *"My son, pay attention to what I say; turn your ear to my words. Do not let them out of your sight, keep them within your heart; for they are life to those who find them and health to one's whole body. Above all else, guard your heart, for everything you do flows from*

it." (Proverbs 4:20-23, NIV)

17. **God brought healing to the world through Jesus:** *"But he was pierced for our transgressions, he was crushed for our iniquities; the punishment that brought us peace was on him, and by his wounds we are healed." (Isaiah 53:5, NIV)*

18. **God heals:** *"'But I will restore you to health and heal your wounds', declares the Lord, 'because you are called an outcast, Zion for whom no one cares.'" (Jeremiah 30:17, NIV)*

19. **God blesses those who honor Him:** *"'Bring the whole tithe into the storehouse, that there may be food in my house. Test me in this,' says the Lord Almighty, 'and see if I will not throw open the floodgates of heaven and pour out so much blessing that there will not be room enough to store it.'" (Malachi 3:10, NIV)*

New Testament Promises:

1. **Jesus performs healing miracles:** *"Jesus went throughout Galilee, teaching in their synagogues, proclaiming the good news of the kingdom, and healing every disease and sickness among the people. News about him spread all over Syria, and people brought to him all who were ill with various diseases, those suffering severe pain, the demon-possessed, those having seizures, and the paralyzed; and he healed them. Large crowds from Galilee, the Decapolis, Jerusalem, Judea and the region across the Jordan followed him." (Matthew 4:23-25, NIV)*

2. **Jesus performs a healing miracle:** *"A man with leprosy came and knelt before him and said, 'Lord, if you are willing, you can make me clean.' Jesus reached out his hand and touched the man. 'I am willing,' he said. 'Be clean!' Immediately he was cleansed of his leprosy." (Matthew 8:2-3, NIV)*

3. **Jesus performs another healing miracle:** *"Then Jesus said to the centurion, 'Go! Let it be done just as you believed it would.' And his servant was healed at that moment." (Matthew 8: 13, NIV)*

4. **Prayer is very powerful:** *"Again, truly I tell you that if two of you on earth agree about anything they ask for, it will be done for them by my Father in heaven." (Matthew 18:19, NIV)*

5. **Faith is essential in prayer:** *"'Have faith in God,' Jesus answered. 'Truly I tell you, if anyone says to this mountain, 'Go, throw yourself into the sea,' and does not doubt in their heart but believes that what*

they say will happen, it will be done for them'." (Mark 11:22-23, NIV)

6. **Belief is essential in prayer:** *"Therefore I tell you, whatever you ask for in prayer, believe that you have received it, and it will be yours."* (Mark 11:24, NIV)

7. **Jesus, through the Holy Spirit, has equipped believers to perform miracles:** *"And these signs will accompany those who believe: In my name they will drive out demons; they will speak in new tongues; they will pick up snakes with their hands; and when they drink deadly poison, it will not hurt them at all; they will place their hands on sick people, and they will get well."* (Mark 16:17-18, NIV)

8. **The Holy Spirit provides life:** *"And if the Spirit of him who raised Jesus from the dead is living in you, he who raised Christ from the dead will also give life to your mortal bodies because of his Spirit who lives in you."* (Romans 8:11, NIV)

9. **God listens to those who believe Him:** *"We know that God does not listen to sinners. He listens to the godly person who does his will."* (John 9:31, NIV)

10. **Jesus provides life:** *"The thief comes only to steal and kill and destroy; I have come that they may have life, and have it to the full."* (John 10:10, NIV)

11. **Hope brings peace:** *"Therefore, since we have been justified through faith, we have peace with God through our Lord Jesus Christ, through whom we have gained access by faith into this grace in which we now stand. And we boast in the hope of the glory of God."* (Romans 5:1-2, NIV)

12. **Jesus is the gateway to all the promises of God:** *"For no matter how many promises God has made, they are "Yes" in Christ. And so through him the "Amen" is spoken by us to the glory of God."* (2 Corinthians 1:20, NIV)

13. **The spirit war is real:** *"The weapons we fight with are not the weapons of the world. On the contrary, they have divine power to demolish strongholds. We demolish arguments and every pretension that sets itself up against the knowledge of God, and we take captive every thought to make it obedient to Christ."* (2 Corinthians 10:4,5, NIV)

14. **Jesus is the only path to God:** *"Christ redeemed us from the curse of the law by becoming a curse for us, for it is written: 'Cursed is everyone who is hung on a pole.' He redeemed us in order that the blessing given to Abraham might come to the Gentiles through Christ Jesus, so that by*

faith we might receive the promise of the Spirit." (Galatians 3:13-14, NIV)

15. **God is with us when we fight in spiritual warfare:** *"Finally, be strong in the Lord and in his mighty power. Put on the full armor of God, so that you can take your stand against the devil's schemes. For our struggle is not against flesh and blood, but against the rulers, against the authorities, against the powers of this dark world and against the spiritual forces of evil in the heavenly realms. Therefore put on the full armor of God, so that when the day of evil comes, you may be able to stand your ground, and after you have done everything, to stand." (Ephesians 6:10-13, NIV)*

16. **God works within us to bring us to Him:** *"for it is God who works in you to will and to act in order to fulfill his good purpose." (Philippians 2:13, NIV)*

17. **The Holy Spirit equips us for life in this earth:** *"For the Spirit God gave us does not make us timid, but gives us power, love and self-discipline." (2 Timothy 1:7, NIV)*

18. **We have Hope in God:** *"Let us hold unswervingly to the hope we profess, for he who promised is faithful." (Hebrews 10:23, NIV)*

19. **Hold strong to the Hope:** *"So do not throw away your confidence; it will be richly rewarded." (Hebrews 10:35, NIV)*

20. **Faith is required for Hope:** *Now faith is confidence in what we hope for and assurance about what we do not see. (Hebrews 11:1, NIV)*

21. **Our Hope in Jesus is forever:** *"Jesus Christ is the same yesterday and today and forever." (Hebrews 13:8, NIV)*

22. **Prayer is vital to overcoming sickness:** *"Is anyone among you sick? Let them call the elders of the church to pray over them and anoint them with oil in the name of the Lord. And the prayer offered in faith will make the sick person well; the Lord will raise them up. If they have sinned, they will be forgiven." (James 5:14-15, NIV)*

23. **Jesus died so that we may be healed:** *"'He himself bore our sins' in his body on the cross, so that we might die to sins and live for righteousness; 'by his wounds you have been healed'." (1 Peter 2:24, NIV)*

24. **We can ask God for anything:** *"Dear friends, if our hearts do not condemn us, we have confidence before God and receive from him anything we ask, because we keep his commands and do what pleases him." (1 John 3:21-22, NIV)*

25. ***God hears us when we pray:*** *"This is the confidence we have in approaching God: that if we ask anything according to his will, he hears us. And if we know that he hears us—whatever we ask—we know that we have what we asked of him." (1 John 5:14-15, NIV)*

26. ***Pray for good health:*** *"Dear friend, I pray that you may enjoy good health and that all may go well with you, even as your soul is getting along well." (3 John 1:2, NIV)*

27. ***God wins:*** *"They triumphed over him by the blood of the Lamb and by the word of their testimony; they did not love their lives so much as to shrink from death." (Revelation 12:11, NIV)*

October 14, 2016

Today I had my third treatment; three more to go. After 9 hours I am feeling better but not totally. I just hate these treatments; barbaric is how I sum them up. When I finish the next three, that will make 23 treatments I have had. Seven were chemo and sixteen were this treatment. I sure do pray that this set will kill all of the cancer.

December 16, 2016

Well, I finished up the last three treatments and had a difficult time with abdominal issues from pain to diarrhea. Saw the doctor about the problem and at first the doctor thought it was diverticulitis and put me on strong antibiotics - this turned out to cause more problems. So then the doctor thought it might be something else and put me on different medicine. I believed it was from the surgery and treatments. About 3 weeks being off treatments I started to feel better and no problem now.

Today I had another cycloscope and it turned out good - bladder looked the best since the cancer was found. Will have another one in three months and if good the doctor said I would do a maintenance treatment (3).

Procrastinating (Roger)

"There is a time for everything, and a season for every activity under the heavens: a time to be born and a time to die, a time to plant and a time to uproot, a time to kill and a time to heal, a time to tear down and a time to build, a time to weep and a time to laugh, a time to mourn and a time to dance, a time to scatter stones and a time to gather them, a time to embrace and a time to refrain from embracing, a time to search and a time to give up, a time to keep and a time to throw away, a time to tear and a time to mend, a time to be silent and a time to speak, a time to love and a time to hate, a time for war and a time for peace." (Ecclesiastes 3:1-8, NIV)

As children, we read this passage and made the mistake of thinking that it applied to household chores: "There is a time to do the dishes but it is not right now as we are watching our favorite TV show". Or, "There is a time to weed the garden and it is not in the morning when the dew makes everything sticky and gross. It is also not the time to weed the garden during the heat of the day because we will sweat to death". Or, our favorite interpretation of Ecclesiastes 3, "There is a time to pull the weeds from the driveway and it is never".

Needless to say, Dad didn't agree with our interpretation of Scripture. The "Gospel of Bruce" was: don't put off until tomorrow what you can do today. Actually, don't even put off until later today what you can do right now. This was a losing theological argument between the kids and the parents because Dad's philosophy was technically rooted in the Bible. The author of Proverbs 6 writes the Warnings Against Folly; of particular relevance to what Dad was teaching us is found in verses 1-11.

Dad adhered to this philosophy for the majority of his life and experiences. Whenever he took on a project, he worked hard to complete it as quickly as possible. If he was going to teach a lesson in Sunday School, he would start working on it early in the week rather than on Saturday night like one of his sons was keen to do (yes, that was me). If there was a chore or project to do around the house, he would get it done as soon as possible after he got home after work or as early as possible on Saturday.

But he wasn't perfect. There were a few facets in life where Dad procrastinated. Overseas travel was one of those areas where he delayed trips that were on his bucket list. He had always wanted to visit the WWII sites at Normandy, France. The military historian in him wanted to personally view the location where D-Day occurred. He wanted to also visit the cemetery there and pay homage to the troops that turned the tide in the European front. On the same trip he planned to visit the "homeland" (The Netherlands) to see where his ancestors originated. But he kept delaying the trip because he did not want to sit in a plane seat for 7+ hours. Unfortunately, he was never able to visit either of these places because of his procrastination.

In most facets of our lives, procrastinating doesn't lead to good outcomes. As we continue to read through Dad's journal, it is clear that the one aspect of his life that he did not procrastinate was visiting doctors when necessary. What would have happened if Dad had continued to wait and put off that nagging voice that he should have his bladder evaluated?

Consider your life: what are you putting off today that requires attention? Perhaps there is an unfinished project in your garage that needs to be completed. Perhaps there is a family member or friend with whom you need to resolve differences and restore the relationship. Perhaps there is a doctor's office where you need to schedule an appointment.

Dad regretted that he didn't visit France and The Netherlands. Don't put yourself in a similar position: don't procrastinate.

2017

New Normal (Roger)

As planet Earth began it's new revolution around the sun on January 1, 2017, Dad had been battling bladder cancer for 27 months. For more than two years he had undergone dozens, if not hundreds, of examinations from a multitude of doctors in a myriad of medical facilities. Despite all of this attention, Dad was still basically living day-to-day. He was waiting for bad news to come from the doctor's office. He was waiting to hear that he needed to do more treatment or to have another surgery to kill the cancer invading his bladder.

When many people use the phrase "new normal", they refer to losing a job, getting divorced, etc. For Dad, it was a process of constant treatment for bladder cancer.

He fought to embrace this new normal despite not having a clear picture of the light at the end of the tunnel. As the calendar moved from 2016 to 2017, he didn't let his illnesses affect his immediate future. He made plans to go on a cruise with Mom to the Caribbean. He continued strengthening his relationships with his grandchildren, including the children of a woman his son was dating. He became more involved with his church in Florida.

But as we have seen before, the universe was not finished with making Dad's life difficult.

February 10, 2017 (Bruce)

It seems only appropriate to start a new chapter with a potential new problem. I had a Wellness checkup with the doctor today. I mentioned that for about 1 ½ weeks I have been having short intense headaches on the left temple around the eye and that sometimes it just hurts to touch the left part of the eye socket. The doctor did not know what the problem might be and suggested I see an eye doctor. Made an appointment.

February 15, 2017

Saw the doctor and explained about the eye problem. The doctor examined the eye and location and was concerned that it might be Temporal Arteritis, a very serious issue. The doctor wanted me to have a couple of blood tests immediately at the local medical facility. The reason to go to this particular medical facility was that the doctor would have the results by the afternoon. Went to the medical facility for the tests, two of them.

Temporal arteritis Highlights

- *Nearly one-quarter million people in the United States have temporal arteritis.*
- *Temporal arteritis is almost nonexistent in people under the age of 50.*
- *Untreated temporal arteritis can lead to other serious conditions, including aneurysms, strokes, and even death.*

Temporal arteritis is a condition in which the temporal arteries, which supply blood to the head and brain, become inflamed or damaged. It is also known as cranial arteritis or giant cell arteritis. Although this condition usually occurs in the temporal arteries, it can occur in almost any medium to large artery in the body.

Although the exact cause of the condition is unknown, it may be linked to the body's autoimmune response. Also, excessive doses of antibiotics and certain severe infections have been linked to temporal arteritis. There's no known prevention. However, once diagnosed, temporal arteritis can be treated to minimize complications.

Sed rate (erythrocyte sedimentation rate)

- *Results from your sed rate test will be reported in the distance in millimeters (mm) that red blood cells have descended in one hour (hr). The normal range is 0-22 mm/hr for men and 0-29 mm/hr for women. The upper threshold for a normal sed rate value may vary somewhat from one medical practice to another.*
- *A number of conditions can affect the properties of blood, thereby affecting how quickly red blood cells sink in a sample of blood. So information about inflammatory disease — what your doctor intends to learn from the sed rate test — can be obscured by the influence of other conditions.*

- *These complicating factors include:*
  - *Advanced age*
  - *Kidney problems*
  - *Thyroid disease*
  - *Some cancers, such as multiple myeloma*

In the afternoon received a call from the doctor and one test, ESR (Erythrocyte Sedimentation Rate), was higher than expected. The doctor wanted me to see a specialist as soon as possible and suggested one to visit. On Feb 17th received a call that the Dr. wanted to see me as soon as I could be worked into his schedule. Normal time for an appointment was toward the end of March. I was scheduled for March 1, 2017.

I think I have said this before but when does the trouble ever stop? How many trials and tests must a person go through? Isn't prostate cancer, bladder cancer, and the other problems I have had sufficient? Should I wear this as another badge on my uniform? Maybe my worries will be for naught and it turns out to be nothing; however, the waiting and visits to different doctors plus the urgency they place on seeing me and having tests done is troublesome.

Hedges (Roger)

"I think I have said this before but when does the trouble ever stop? How many trials and tests must a person go through? Isn't prostate cancer, bladder cancer, and the other problems I have had sufficient?"

When Dad wrote the above, it was from a point of despair because he had just learned that his body was, yet again, failing him. With no clear end in sight, he was unable to reflect on all the blessings that God had provided throughout his life. He came from a loving family and was blessed to walk with God early in his life which enabled Dad to also create his own loving family. He had not one but two highly successful careers. He was an avid volunteer, sacrificing his time and resources to assist others. He was truly a blessed man, except that the hedge protecting him from physical disease and illness had become porous.

Early in the book of Job, the word "hedge" is used to describe God's protection in Job's life. The devil challenges God about Job that, "Have you not put a hedge around him and his household and everything he has?" (Job 1:10, NIV).

The implication to the challenge is similar to saying that the only reason people love God is because He blesses them with good life. The devil was basically saying that God is like a kid that offers candy so that other kids will like him or her. This is not accurate: God puts up hedges in our life to protect us from more than we can bear. God is in control of these hedges.

Throughout his struggles, Dad was drawn to the story of Job because he could identify with Job's crisis of faith as described in the Bible. The book begins by describing Job's wealth and position of prominence in the land of Uz. Job was described as a man that was "blameless and upright; he feared God and shunned evil" and that Job was the "greatest man among all the people of the East" (Job 1:1,3, NIV).

In verses 9-11, the devil questioned whether Job's faith was real or whether it was the result of God's blessings on Job. The insinuation is that without all of the blessings of God, Job would walk away from his faith. So God removed the "hedge" of protection and the devil tested Job in the following manners:

- Test #1: "The Lord said to satan, 'Very well, then, everything he has is in your power, but on the man himself do not lay a finger'" (Job 1:12, NIV). After this, Job lost his livestock, his servants, and many of his sons and daughters. Yet despite all of this tragedy, despite all of the losses that he had incurred, Job refused to curse and turn his back on God.
- Test #2: "The Lord said to satan, 'Very well, then, he is in your hands; but you must spare his life'" (Job 2:6, NIV). After this conversation, the devil afflicted Job with "painful sores from the soles of his feet to the crown of his head." (Verse 7, NIV). Again, despite all of his suffering, Job refused to curse and turn his back on God.

The remainder of the book is a story of how Job curses everything, including his lot in life, but does not curse God. Although the hedge of protection had been removed from his well-being and the lives of his relatives, Job did not curse God.

The book of Job tells us that no matter what we think about our experiences in life, God has placed the hedges in our lives at the correct location. We may not like or even agree with his plan, but we need to remember that He is God and that we are not. The hedges are in that exact spot for a reason.

As we experience struggles and strife, it would be good for us to consider the following about hedges:

1. Truth #1: Hedges are Biblical. In the book of Job, God doesn't deny the existence of the hedge when the devil challenges God. The Bible is full of stories that demonstrate that God has placed a hedge around His people. Consider the stories of Moses, Joseph, Daniel, and Jonah in the Old Testament. Consider the numerous times in the New Testament that the Apostle Paul is either thrown in jail or in a shipwreck but still survives to accomplish God's Plan. Today, God continues this work and has established hedges of protection for believers. Where has God established His protection around you?

2. Truth #2: Hedges are movable. In the story of Job, notice that God allows the hedge around Job to be moved from the external realm (family, wealth, well-being) to simply a hedge around Job's physical body. This is important to us as we go through struggles because if a hedge can be moved, then someone must be capable of doing the moving. Where can you ask God to expand His hedge of protection around you?

3. Truth #3: We can pray for these hedges to be adjusted. If hedges are created by God and God can move the hedges, then it makes sense that we can pray to God to have our hedges moved. In college, one of the most-talked about college classes was the Old Testament Introduction class where the professor, the late, great Dr. Wilbur Williams, spoke of the power and mercy of God to move hedges to protect us from the evil one. The class was designed for incoming Freshmen to hear early on in our college career that God protects us. This was very reassuring and this same message continues to resonate with me all these years later.

4. Truth #4: We can pray for the hedges of our friends and family. If we can pray to God and ask the Creator of the universe to move our hedges, doesn't it make sense that we can also pray an intercessory prayer for our loved ones? Who in your life is going through a difficult circumstance and can benefit from God's protection?

Even though man's fall created separation between us and God, He continues to love us. In His mercy, He provides protection for us from life's injustices and cruelties. He doesn't promise that life will be perfect. But He has promised to be with us during our struggles.

March 1, 2017 (Bruce)

Saw the doctor today about my eye. The doctor did several tests and could not rule out Temporal Arteritis, or also called Giant Cell Arteritis ("GCA"). Therefore I have been scheduled for surgery on March 6, 2017, at 2:30pm at a local medical facility.

The doctor gave me a pamphlet on Temporal Arteritis and I have been doing some research on my own as well on the Internet. The good news is that this will not kill me. But the bad news is that if I have it, life will be considerably less enjoyable. Some of my findings include the following:

- *GCA is a condition where an inflammation can actually destroy blood vessels or arteries.*
- *GCA is generally found in people over the age of 60.*
- *GCA has the potential to significantly damage the optic nerve because the inflammation constricts the flow of necessary blood supply. The result is irreversible loss of vision.*
- *GCA sometimes manifests itself as headaches or other pains in the head area.*
- *Once a GCA is suspected, immediate intervention is necessary to stop further vision loss.*
- *Blood work panel is the typical diagnostic procedure but tests are entirely forthright, which puts the onus on the doctor for early suspicion and detection.*

- If a GCA is suspected, then a biopsy should be scheduled as soon as possible.
- Treatment is possible; drugs are used to manage the condition.

March 6, 2017

Had my surgery today at a local medical facility. Arrived at 1:15pm but did not have surgery until around 4:45pm. Was in surgery room for about 1 hour but was told the surgery took about 25 minutes. Then I was placed in the recovery room and left about 6:00pm.

March 14, 2017

Well recovery was going well until around 1:00p on Thursday, March 9, 2017. At that time I still had not had a bowel movement and started to have pains and the pressure to have a bowel movement but could not. At about 2:30 pm I told Donna that we needed to go to a medical facility as the pain was terrible.

At the medical facility I was immediately given attention after registering. After several tests etc they inserted a tube in my nose, down my throat and into my stomach in order to pump it out and relieve pressure on my small intestine. This remained in me until about noon the following day. I have had several surgeries but this ordeal has been by far the most painful. I received 4 pain killer shots. At about 3:15am on Friday I finally had a good bowel movement. This was a tremendous relief. Eventually I was discharged around 4:00pm on Friday. The official diagnosis was a small bowel obstruction.

March 18, 2017

Well, I continued to have limited bowel movements until today. I have been taking a drug and eating/drinking a lot of prune material. Still not back to normal but better.

On March 14, 2017, I saw a doctor about the eye biopsy. It was negative. Thank you God as Temporal Arteritis is a serious condition. The doctor believes the problem now resides in the nerve/tendon in the back of the head at the base. Could be caused by tension or some other issues. I saw another doctor on Wed, March 15, 2017, and the doctor said this is a common problem with a lot of people and recommended not doing anything at this time (I have not had headaches for past two weeks).

In the morning on March 17, 2017, I saw the doctor for my three-month bladder cancer evaluation. My PSA was negative (no recurrence of prostate *cancer). The doctor did a cystoscope and saw no tumors but a few small red areas, however, not sufficient to do a biopsy. The doctor is going to do three maintenance treatments starting March 31st for three weeks.*

So, all in all this has been a good week. Again, thank you God and for all those who offered prayers.

Distractions and Diversions (Roger)

On March 19th, Mom and Dad drove to Miami, FL for a one-night hotel stay because they did not want to be late to board a cruise ship the next morning. The cruise was a ten-day jaunt around various islands in the Caribbean, some of which they had previously visited and some that were new. They enjoyed everything about cruises: the food, the entertainment on the ship, visiting new places, and meeting new people. They even went on shore excursions from time to time. But mostly they enjoyed being removed from the distractions of the "mainland".

This was not their first cruise but this particular cruise was different from past cruises because it provided a big distraction from Dad's battle with bladder cancer. Was Dad symptom-free during this cruise? Of course not, but neither was he visiting multiple doctors' offices during those ten days. Dad liked to document the cruises and created a photo-book of each cruise. The photos of this cruise showed that Dad was able to disconnect himself from the disease; he and Mom had a great time on this cruise.

Life during this period of time was a challenge for Dad. Early in his military career he learned the value of distractions when he was able to fly from Vietnam to Hawaii for his R&R time (Rest and Relaxation). When he was working in his career, he was adamant that the family would travel for a 1-2 week summer vacation. He called every couple of days (from a pay phone) to ensure that the office hadn't burned down, but for the most part, he put work out of his mind. He knew that the vacation was a necessary distraction from the stresses of life.

Distractions and diversions are important to all of us as we navigate through the stresses of our lives. It should come as no surprise to learn that they are also based in scripture, including in the life of Jesus.

Too often, we think of the picture of Jesus smiling as He welcomed children into His presence. But we need to remember that Jesus was fully human, just like you and me. Was Jesus welcoming 100% of the time? Likely not. It seems reasonable to believe that His humanness required time to withdraw and recharge. There are numerous instances of Jesus withdrawing himself from the people so that he could pray. In Mark 6, we read the following:

"The apostles gathered around Jesus and reported to him all they had done and taught. Then, because so many people were coming and going that they did not even have a chance to eat, he said to them, 'Come with me by yourselves to a quiet place and get some rest.' So they went away by themselves in a boat to a solitary place." (Mark 6:30-32, NIV)

In reality, our struggles are not as severe as those Jesus was going through during His time on earth; He literally had the weight of the world on His shoulders. But the challenges are significant for each of us, especially those among us who are facing life and death medical issues like Dad. But it's important that we seek out these distractions and diversions; they are therapeutic by:

- Getting our minds off the nitty-gritty of the struggle. Whether you're snoozing in a hammock on a beach, visiting a museum in another city, or literally thousands of other possibilities, it's going to be a challenge to ignore your surroundings and focus on your struggle. While on the cruise, Dad spent infinitely more time reading a book or learning about a new country than he did worrying about his next test.
- Allowing us to spend focused time with relatives, friends, and acquaintances. Dad and Mom usually went on cruises with family members and were able to build memories together.
- And most importantly, providing an opportunity for us to reflect on God's majesty. I am writing this section of the book during the 4th of July holiday. We went to the beach to watch fireworks on the evening of the 4th and were fortunate to select a location where we could see fireworks all along the coastline, from city to city. This was a welcome distraction

from a struggle that I am currently fighting. However, what was even more of a diversion was a thunderstorm offshore with a lightning show that vastly outmatched the fireworks. As I watched the lightning show and marveled at God's creation, my thoughts did not focus on my struggle even a single moment.

What can be your distraction or diversion? Your distraction doesn't have to be a ten-day cruise. It could be as simple as a weekend away, a day away, or even a long drive. I recently went on a 29-hour holiday in a town about 2 hours north of my house to get distracted. As I spent time on the beach, resting and relaxing, never once did I think about the stresses of life. When I returned home and went back to work, I was refreshed and my attitude towards others had improved.

What can be your distraction? When can you go?

April 14, 2017 (Bruce)

Well I finished up my third maintenance treatment yesterday. It was in the afternoon. Not so much trouble this time compared with the second treatment. Still was not pleasant. As of now I have had 26 treatments for the bladder cancer.

The doctor also wanted a CT scan of the bladder and kidneys so that was done last Monday at a local medical facility. The results were negative which was very good news. Means the cancer has not spread up the tubes into the kidneys.

Go back June 23, 2017, for another cystoscopy.

June 23, 2017

Had my scope today. The doctor did not see any visible cancer, but some redness which could also be due to the treatment. Need to have another scope Sept 22, 2017, and also I need to have an in-depth look at a urine sample for cancer cells. Basically same results and next steps as last year in June. It has been 2 ½ years since they found the bladder cancer and I am still alive and actually feel pretty good. However, the cloud is still over my head and no matter which direction I move, the cloud moves in the same direction. Sometimes it rains.

July 25, 2017

Praise God for His goodness. My urine test for cancer cells came back negative. No cancer cells detected. This is the first break in the cycle since 2014 of dealing with bladder cancer. No surgery this summer! Next test, scope, is Sept 22, 2017.

Family (Roger)

Missing from Dad's journal were descriptions and accounts of family life. He described a few family events earlier in the journal, but mostly these were included to provide context for the onset of a medical issue. There are very few instances of family dinners, trips, activities, etc.

Why didn't he include these events? Perhaps he didn't want to call attention to himself. More likely the reason is that Dad didn't think it was a big deal that his family had a strong bond and enjoyed being together. But it is a big deal. How would our society look with stronger family relationships? Would happiness levels increase or decrease? How about stress levels? Suicide rates? Would crime increase or decrease?

Dad made a few comments in his journal about not spending enough time with family during his working years. This was probably one of his greatest regrets. He spent countless nights in hotels as he visited crime labs throughout the state of Illinois. He spent one weekend a month and two weeks during the summer fulfilling his commitment to the National Guard. There was also at least one elder's meeting at church every month, meetings that lasted well into the night.

But here's the thing about regret: Dad's regret didn't allow him to realize that we understood that his commitment to providing for the family resulted in difficult decisions. We understood his dilemma. We accepted his decision and forgave him because we knew it was all done with love. Were we upset when he didn't make it to a sporting event, a band concert, or a Bible Bowl tournament? Sure. But did we hold it against him for years or decades afterwards? No. We knew that he was making the correct, but tough, choice to earn a living so that the needs of the family were met.

After he retired, he spent a lot of time with not only his nuclear family, but his extended family as well. He conversed with his brother more frequently than ever before in their adult lives. He spent countless hours working on home improvement projects with his son and his brother-in-law. He poured himself into creating meaningful relationships with his grandchildren. It is reasonable to believe that he was making up for time lost during his career years.

He continued putting family first until the day that he passed on to the next life. His journal doesn't mention it, but he put his health struggles behind him and focused on family. In the later half of 2017, his time was spent focusing on family:

- May: Attended grand-daughter's dance recital. Drove from Northern Illinois to Minneapolis to help his son (the author of this book) to look for apartments as he was considering selling his house. Dad and Mom found a nice apartment in the same suburb and secured a contract for the rental.

- June: Drove back up to the Minneapolis area to assist with the son's move. Dad and Mom actually did most of the packing, especially the kitchen and garage, which were packing nightmares. Without their assistance, the move would have been a big challenge.

- July & August: Established relationships with the children of a woman his other son was seriously dating. These children would eventually become his step-grandchildren and loved him deeply.

- September: Evacuated his newly purchased house in Florida due to the threat of hurricane Irma and spent time in Alabama to avoid the storm (more on that later).

- October: Participated as the Best Man to his son's wedding. Partied like a rock star during the reception.

- November: Counseled his son (author) after a break-up with his lady friend. He was gracious. He even put up with my abnormal requests such as don't drive on a certain side of the community where they lived because that was where she lived. This request aggravated him but he never said no, at least to my knowledge.

Dad was the embodiment of prioritizing and improving the health of the family unit. He strove to repair all family relationships by showing love to all. He spent as much time as possible with family because he believed the old adage that says no one on their death bed says "I wish I had spent more time in the office."

The Bible is full of passages that speak to the importance of strong relationships between family members. There are passages to children about obeying parents, to parents about loving their children, to husbands about loving their wives, to wives about supporting their husbands, and many other passages. Two that speak directly to the need for a strong family relationship are Ephesians 4:1-3 and Galatians 6:2

How is your relationship with your family? Is there a relationship that needs to be repaired? Don't procrastinate: start the work today to restore the relationship.

August 11, 2017 (Bruce)

Biked 12 miles in the morning prior to breakfast and after returning started to develop pain in lower left abdomen; came on rather quickly. Had some nausea and sweats. Very similar to what I had experienced on May 12, 2015. Pain intensified, about an 8-9, and around 11:30 went to a local medical facility. They did blood and urine tests plus CT. Had blood in the urine. CT showed some diverticulitis but no infection. Possible kidney stone. Afterwards have had some discomfort but not pain.

August 15, 2017

Received news today of two skin biopsies I had done on August 10, 2017. One was on my left forearm and the other was on my forehead-near left center. The result of the left forearm was pre-cancer so I need to go back for a liquid nitrogen freezing treatment. The one on the forehead was positive for basal cell. I have been scheduled for surgery on the 28th of August.

August 31, 2017

Well had my surgery for Basal Cell Cancer on Monday, August 28, 2017. Took out a circle about size of a quarter and then stitched it up both on inside and outside. Seven stitches on outside as they drew the skin together. Also had another biopsy done on cheek below left ear. Today received a call that it was positive for squamous cell cancer and surgery is scheduled for September 18, 2017.

Good Samaritans (Roger)

Summer is the rainy season in Southwest Florida (SWFL) and the year 2017 was particularly rainy: Many of the ditches and water retention ponds were nearing capacity as July turned into August. Dad and Mom had just moved into a new house in a gated community where 95% of the homes are on a pond and were justifiably worried about the rising water.

To make matters worse, when Hurricane Harvey made its way through the Gulf of Mexico towards Texas, the rain bands sat over SWFL for days on end. The water was definitely on the minds of anyone that had a house near any type of water.

Dad was worried about whether their new house would be flooded from excess water from the retention pond behind the house. His fears increased when Hurricane Harvey made its way into the Gulf of Mexico and headed towards Texas because rain bands parked over Southwestern Florida for multiple days. By the end of August, water was everywhere.

I was in town visiting Mom and Dad over Labor Day. The amount of water on the ground was impressive: The retention ponds in their community had rarely been higher. To make matters worse, when I was leaving town, the weather forecasters began commenting on a new tropical wave off the coast of Africa. The projected path was similar to the previous storm that hit SWFL several years prior and we had a feeling of unease that this storm would also affect this area.

As the storm neared the US, the projected path was either SWFL or the eastern coast of Florida. The storm had a name by this time, Irma, and was gaining strength every day. This was their first experience with a cyclonic storm and there were numerous concerns that Dad and Mom were weighing:

- Flooding: A massive amount of rainfall from the storm would lead to catastrophic flooding because all of the water control measures (ponds, ditches, etc.) were already over capacity due to the rain dumped from Hurricane Harvey.

- Strength: The weather forecasters were predicting a Category 3 storm but ratings of 4 and 5 were also a possibility. The stronger the storm, the higher the damage.

- Wind: Trusted friends with hurricane experience were confident that Mom and Dad's house would stand with Category 3 winds but that they shouldn't take a chance with anything higher. Winds of a Category 4 or 5 storm are among the most devastating on the planet.

- Storm Surge: Destruction was also projected to the area from a storm surge. The storm surge is basically a low-grade tsunami: the hurricane forces ocean water miles inland, wiping out anything in its path. Forecasters were projecting that the storm surge had the potential to reach Mom and Dad's community, approximately 8 miles from the coast.

- Power Grid: Hurricanes generally destroy power lines, leaving the affected area without power for days, if not weeks. If Irma hit SWFL, Mom and Dad faced the potential of several days without power, most notably air conditioning.

Dad and Mom weighed all these options and held multiple discussions with friends that had lived through previous hurricanes. The feeling was that it would be acceptable to stay in their home if the storm was a Category 3 but that they should evacuate if Irma looked to hit at a 4 or 5 rating. As the storm neared the US, the forecasters still were not sure how powerful the storm would be when it hit Florida. When their minister decided to leave with his family, Dad and Mom decided to evacuate.

They made the drive north out of the state. The highways were full of people leaving SWFL ahead of IRMA. After making its way through the Florida Keys, Irma made landfall on September 10th in Collier County, which was just south of Mom and Dad's community. Although it made land as a Category 3 storm, it was a strong Cat 3 storm. The path of the storm was very close to Dad and Mom's community; it actually was directly over their sister/brother-in-law's community. Hindsight is always 20/20, but in retrospect, they made the correct decision.

As they continued to drive out of the path of the storm, they faced uncertainty as they listened to the weather reports of the storm's progress. Would they make it out of Florida in time before the hurricane hit? Would their home be standing when they came back? Where would they go? Would they run out of gas before they got to a suitable destination?

Dad and Mom made it as far as Lake City, FL the first night. From there they drove to Alabama and selected the town of Florence, AL, as their home base during the evacuation. Evidently they were not the only Floridians seeking refuge in Florence: there were many evacuees staying in the town. So many in fact that the hotel clerk told them that the area churches got together and divided the hotels among the churches so that they could help with the evacuees. The hospitality shown to all the evacuees was tremendous:

- Churches provided pizza for people staying at the hotels.
- The churches also provided crafts and an activity for the children in the hotel's conference room.
- A patron paid for their lunch at one of the local restaurants
- Bags of supplies (snacks, food, wipes, and water) were left in the hotel lobby for evacuees to take.
- When they left the evacuees were provided with a gas card, a gift card, and cash for their journey back to Florida.

When they arrived back in their community, they found moderate amounts of wind damage, some localized flooding, and the power was off. The same was true for their sister / brother-in-law's house: they were also fortunate to have minor damage. They all realized that they were very fortunate: many people in SWFL were not as lucky. Dad and Mom tried to help as many people as possible to overcome the storm damage.

Irma was yet another curve-ball thrown Dad's way by the universe. But it didn't even phase him. Dad didn't even make a note in his journal of their leaving home, the clean-up, no power when they got back home, etc. But the generosity of the people in Florence, AL, made a big impact on Dad and Mom.

"On one occasion an expert in the law stood up to test Jesus. 'Teacher,' he asked, 'what must I do to inherit eternal life?' 'What is written in the Law?' he replied. 'How do you read it?' He answered, 'Love the Lord your God with all your heart and with all your soul and with all your strength and with all your mind'; and, 'Love your neighbor as yourself.' 'You have answered correctly,' Jesus replied. 'Do this and you will live.' But he wanted to justify himself, so he asked Jesus, 'And who is my neighbor?' In reply Jesus said: 'A man was going down from Jerusalem to Jericho, when he was attacked by robbers. They stripped him of his clothes, beat him and went away, leaving him half dead. A priest happened to be going down the same road, and when he saw the man, he passed by on the other side. So too, a Levite, when he came to the place and saw him, passed by on the other side. But a Samaritan, as he traveled, came where the man was; and when he saw him, he took pity on him. He went to him and bandaged his wounds, pouring on oil and wine. Then he put the man on his own donkey, brought him to an inn and took care of him. The next day he took out two denarii and gave them to the innkeeper. 'Look after him,' he said, 'and when I return, I will reimburse you for any extra expense you may have.' 'Which of these three do you think was a neighbor to the man who fell into the hands of robbers?' The expert in the law replied, 'The one who had mercy on him.' Jesus told him, 'Go and do likewise.'" (Luke 10:25-37, NIV)

The citizens of Florence did not have to provide any assistance but they chose to stop and make time for Dad and Mom and the many thousands of other Florida evacuees. Most of the people of Florence probably didn't even meet the evacuees that they had helped. But that's kind of the point, right? We are called to be good Samaritans not to feed our ego, but to help others that are in desperate times of need.

To whom in your life can you be a good Samaritan today?

September 18, 2017 (Bruce)

Had my surgery for Squamous cell cancer on left cheek below ear. Took out about same amount as before, about 11 stitches which includes the inside stitches. Afterwards not as painful as the previous one on my forehead.

September 22, 2017

Today I had my Cystoscopy of the bladder. The doctor saw one area that was red (looked like the end of a skin tag) and plans on doing a biopsy of it on Sept 27, 2017. And we go on and on and on.

September 27, 2017

Had the biopsy of the bladder today. The doctor took three samples and called them fingers hanging from the wall of the bladder. Not a pleasant procedure, particularly when the doctor cauterized the areas where the samples were located. Will hear results next week. Praying for some positive news!

September 28, 2017

Had a colonoscopy this morning. Terrible going through the prep the day before. Only liquids to drink and did not get to sleep until 2:00a with waking up at 5:40a today. Procedure went very well with it looking good except for small amount of diverticulitis. No polyps. Praise God for the great news. Praying that the bladder will be the same.

October 4, 2017

Had an ECHO and Nuclear Stress Test today as ordered by the doctor. Did not like the ECHO as the doctor really pressed hard on the rib cage around the heart. I did not do the Treadmill for the stress test but had the chemical inducement. It was ok, not bad. They let me go home so must not had been real bad results.

October 5, 2017(a)

Met with the doctor this morning at 7:15am in reference to my biopsy results. Not good news as they were positive for cancer. The doctor said it was a different type of cancer but high grade, and only surface. Because high grade the doctor wants to do another surgery which will be in November. He is not sure what type of follow up treatment as the doctor believes the treatment is not working as well as it should be. The doctor will consult with a cancer facility to come up with treatment plan; there are a few alternatives.

This was a little disconcerting particularly about treatment not working like it should. Hope we are not running out of good options.

God's Intervention, not coincidence!

After hearing of the disturbing news from the doctor this morning, I had an elders' meeting. I was rather quiet at the meeting as my mind was not on the elders' issues but on the fact that my cancer had returned. One of the elders caught up with me in the hallway and asked if everything was ok as I was very quiet in the meeting. Although my usual response is generally one of "doing well," I replied that my cancer had returned and required another operation and treatment was unknown because of past failures. I said it was disconcerting. The elder, and more importantly a friend, immediately asked if he could pray for me right then in the hallway. I said yes.

Everyday Evangelism (Roger)

The term "Everyday Evangelism" was coined during a home-made video made by me and fellow students for a ministry class in college. The video was a parody of the skit "Wayne's World" and the purpose was to present ways Christians could evangelize to people not of the Christian faith in our daily life. The video was definitely cringe-worthy; we were after all a bunch of immature college underclassmen. But the content of the video was solid: Everyday we are presented with opportunities to be the light of Christ to others.

Every. Day.

Previously we discussed the importance of stepping outside of our own struggles and providing encouragement to others. Encouragement is an important part of Everyday Evangelism. Little things were big things to Dad. Sending a card to someone is a little thing but it was a big thing to Dad. They helped buoy his spirits when all of the news he was getting on the medical front was bad. He was so touched that he kept all of the cards he received during his struggles. This act of encouragement from people helped to remind Dad that God was in control through their kind words.

Everyday Evangelism can be characterized by acts of encouragement, but there are so many more aspects beyond encouragement. The basic question is this: "How can you show Christ's love to others, especially those who don't know Him"? The goal is to show Christ's light through your actions and life. It is a process of taking a moment and stepping out from under our own struggles and focus on someone else. Would it surprise you to know that it is scriptural?

"You are the salt of the earth. But if the salt loses its saltiness, how can it be made salty again? It is no longer good for anything, except to be thrown out and trampled underfoot. You are the light of the world. A town built on a hill cannot be hidden. Neither do people light a lamp and put it under a bowl. Instead they put it on its stand, and it gives light to everyone in the house. In the same way, let your light shine before others, that they may see your good deeds and glorify your Father in heaven." (Matthew 5:13-16, NIV)

What are some little things that you can do today to be an encouragement to others? How about any of the following?

- Pay for someone in the line behind you at a fast food drive-thru restaurant.
- Bring a meal to a housebound widow or widower.
- Lift your head up when you're walking and say "Good Morning", "Good Afternoon", or "Good Evening" to passersby. Acknowledge, rather than ignore, people.
- Visit someone you know that is in the hospital.
- Check in on an elderly person in your neighborhood.
- Talk to someone in the hallway at work or church. Ask "How are you doing?" Then actually listen to them. Then ask "How can I help" or "How can I pray for you?" This takes only approximately 10 minutes out of the 1,440 minutes of your day, which calculates to 0.7% of your day. Totally worth it to the other person.

Ultimately, we are made stronger in our struggle when we take the focus off ourselves and help someone else. Or at least try to provide hope to someone else.

How will you engage in Everyday Evangelism today?

———————————————————

October 25, 2017 (Bruce)

Donna and I had lunch today with pastor and his wife. This is not a routine lunch, but the pastor's wife asked if we could have lunch before we left for Florida. Upon leaving the pastor offered a positive note of encouragement and said it was going to be ok.

October 26, 2017(a)

Donna and I had just stopped at a Loves Truck Stop off I-39 in Lasalle-Peru, IL when my cell phone rang. It was a friend from Florida. He has called a couple of times in the past few weeks just to see how I am doing. Another voice of encouragement in the darkest of times.

October 26, 2017(b)

Reading a book by Mary C. Neal, MD titled "To Heaven and Back". In the book she speaks about the dichotomy in our life between knowing the good things of God and difficulties. There is a link between suffering and joy; my summation of the section is that without suffering, we would not be able to experience joy and to follow God's command of rejoicing in all circumstances.

As I reflect on her comments, I feel somewhat ashamed that I have been having a "pity party" about my condition instead of looking for the good that can come out of the circumstance. At this writing I do not know what the "good" is going to be: whether it be personal or by having a positive influence on others. Either way, I need to "rejoice" that the experience can be a positive and not a negative. However, I need to also make a choice in the matter as to what it will be.

Importance of a Positive Attitude (Roger)

Experts disagree on almost everything. For example: for every expert that swears by the power of red wine to fight cancer and other diseases, there is one who swears that red wine contributes to the growth of diseases.

However, there is one thing that most experts agree on and that is the power of a positive attitude when we face adversity. No matter the circumstance, the odds of getting to the other side greatly increase if your mind is in a good place. Being hopeful in the potential of the future is so important. Drowning in debt? Create a vision of where you want to be financially and make a positive plan to get there. Trapped in a relationship filled with strife? Be positive and be the change you want to see in the other person. Struggling through illness or sickness? Be positive you'll get through it and move forward accordingly.

Attitude is extremely important. There are many books written to assist with the process of shifting the focus towards positivity. One of the longest lasting, and best selling, books is "The Power of Positive Thinking" by Norman Vincent Peale. As of this writing, the book has been on the market nearly 70 years! Simply written, the book encourages people to make changes in their mind if they want to change their life. The book has been translated into many languages and has helped millions of people transform their lives. We would all do well to purchase a copy, read it on a regular basis, and implement its teaching into our lives. Based on the preceding journal entry, Dad would have benefited from reading this book often during his struggle with bladder cancer.

The challenge to have a positive mindset is the "How": How can we wake up each day with a positive attitude? How can we remain positive to those we interact with during the day, especially as we are struggling? How can we be positive when we go to sleep at night not knowing what tomorrow holds?

One powerful method to answering the "How" question is to count our blessings. I introduced my neighbor in the first book of this series. He is without a doubt the most positive person I have ever met (this is the same neighbor who asks me about how many people are coming to my pity party when my attitude is negative). We have discussed many times where his positive attitude originates. A large part of his positive attitude is recognizing the blessings in life that he has received. He came from a working-class background and has realized that each step in his life was a blessing. He made the conscious decision to help others navigate their day through his positivity. We have enjoyed many a meal at a restaurant where he interacts with complete strangers to brighten their day.

Being positive is important not only for us, but for those around us. As we navigate through the struggles of life, we are not the only ones struggling with negativity. Our friends, families, and acquaintances are also right there with us. We need to be positive for them as well. Two negative people will not result in positivity. But one positive person has the potential to turn the negative person towards positivity.

Have you considered counting your blessings?

For believers, the number one blessing is that God is in our life and has promised to bless us. There are many scriptures that outline this promise. One of the earliest promises is found in the book of Numbers in the Old Testament:

"The Lord said to Moses, 'Tell Aaron and his sons, 'This is how you are to bless the Israelites. Say to them: 'The Lord bless you and keep you; the Lord make his face shine on you and be gracious to you; the Lord turn his face toward you and give you peace.'" (Numbers 6:24-26, NIV)

There is a song on Crowder's "I Know a Ghost" album that maps out a potential path to a positive attitude. The song is entitled "Everyday I'm Blessed" and it is an awesome reminder that God doesn't just bless us once and walk away. No, He continues to bless us everyday. It is important that we acknowledge and reflect on the eternal difference in our lives that God provides to us through His blessings of grace and mercy. When we are a part of His family, despite the struggles of today, we are secure in the certainty that we will be with Him forever.

The title of Crowder's song reminds me of an exercise we used to do in college: How is your life, right now, blessed? How are you blessed everyday? As I write this section, my "blessings inventory" includes the following:

- Blessed to wake up today.
- Blessed to be born again.
- Blessed to have a loving family, including a repaired relationship with my brother whom I didn't treat the best while we were growing up.
- Blessed to have the means to be able to eat and sleep indoors.
- Blessed to be a part of a loving and supportive church family.
- Blessed to live in a country where freedom is present rather than a dream.

Too often I have to remind myself that every day I'm blessed. Every. Day. But forgetting these blessings seems to be easy because it is the result of sin and distance from God. Rather than focusing on Him and all He has done for us, we focus on ourselves. When you conduct the blessings inventory you realize that you are truly blessed. When you come to this realization, it is difficult to NOT have a positive attitude in spite of all of circumstances and the struggles of life.

Life is tough. It is often a struggle. But we are blessed beyond what we deserve. Still not convinced? Open your favorite concordance and search for all the blessings from God that are listed in the Bible. Then make a list of the blessings in your life and see how it affects your positivity.

What is your "Blessings Inventory"?

November 4, 2017 (Bruce)

I am writing this now after my surgery on October 31st, 2017. This was my fourth bladder cancer surgery since I found out about the cancer in November 2014. I was at the medical facility at 11:30 am and was quickly taken into the pre-op area to get prepped. However, I did not go into surgery until about 2:45 pm and was back into a post-op room around 4:45 pm and Donna could come in.

My surgery was called: Cystourethroscopy with Transurethral Resection of the bladder tumor with Fulguration and Mitomycin. Basically what happened is that the doctor applied a high frequency electrical current to destroy any lesions that are present in the bladder.

I do not recall that I had ever had Fulguration; I did receive the chemotherapy on another occasion immediately after a previous surgery.

My recovery this time seems to go better with fewer issues afterwards. The catheter was removed Friday morning. I also did not have any constipation issues, which had always been a major problem for me with past surgeries. Possibly this is because I did not take any narcotic pain reliever (used over the counter medicine) and immediately took a laxative and fiber and prune juice.

At least my mental state is better now; it always is after the surgery, but it was not good this time prior to the surgery. I thank God for seeing me through the surgery and pray that results are going to be good.

As always, Roger and Jamie, have been really good about checking on my condition and calling prior to the surgery.

Author's Note (Roger)

Some might frown on the next section because it can be found in one of the first sections of this book. But it is important to read through this writing at the exact moment of time when Dad actually wrote the passage because it provides context to the words on the page. He was sitting at his computer, six days after his fourth bladder cancer surgery, likely wondering how many more surgeries was it going to take to defeat the cancer?

Dad's journey was not an easy one as you've read throughout this book (and the first book if you read it). However, despite all of his struggles against everything that life had thrown at him, Bruce chose to put pen to paper and write an essay called "He will not fail us".

Context is important. Consider what Dad's mindset could have been in November, 2017, after three years of fighting bladder cancer, not to mention 8 years after being diagnosed with prostate cancer. He could have been bitter, angry, or withdrawn from the world. But he wasn't in any of these negative states of mind. Instead, he chose to cling to God and the promise that this life is fleeting and there is a better life coming.

"He will not fail us" (Bruce)

Psalm 91 (NIV)

> *1 Whoever dwells in the shelter of the Most High*
> *   will rest in the shadow of the Almighty.*
> *2 I will say of the Lord, "He is my refuge and my fortress,*
> *   my God, in whom I trust."*
> *3 Surely he will save you*
> *   from the fowler's snare*
> *   and from the deadly pestilence.*

4 *He will cover you with his feathers,*
  and under his wings you will find refuge;
  his faithfulness will be your shield and rampart.
5 *You will not fear the terror of night,*
  nor the arrow that flies by day,
6 *nor the pestilence that stalks in the darkness,*
  nor the plague that destroys at midday.
7 *A thousand may fall at your side,*
  ten thousand at your right hand,
  but it will not come near you.
8 *You will only observe with your eyes*
  and see the punishment of the wicked.
9 *If you say, "The Lord is my refuge,"*
  and you make the Most High your dwelling,
10 *no harm will overtake you,*
   no disaster will come near your tent.
11 *For he will command his angels concerning you*
   to guard you in all your ways;
12 *they will lift you up in their hands,*
   so that you will not strike your foot against a stone.
13 *You will tread on the lion and the cobra;*
   you will trample the great lion and the serpent.
14 *"Because he loves me," says the Lord, "I will rescue him;*
   I will protect him, for he acknowledges my name.
15 *He will call on me, and I will answer him;*
   I will be with him in trouble,
   I will deliver him and honor him.
16 *With long life I will satisfy him*
   and show him my salvation."

(Bruce) *I am always amazed when those who have cancer outwardly appear to have a tranquil nature. I wish I could copy that DNA of tranquility into my own mind and personality. Maybe they are at peace with their situation and the outward appearance is real and not a brave front. Unfortunately, my situation has been displayed as that of a chameleon. To others I change my color to reflect an appearance of strength and acceptance. I try not to take the cancer seriously in* front of others and when asked I reply, "I'm doing ok". I live a life externally of pretending that nothing really is wrong and a philosophy of "this too will pass - no big deal".

But it is a big deal; I just do not want to admit it outwardly. Besides, I have found that many people who have not experienced the trials of cancer do not want to talk about it, do not understand the emotions a person goes through, may even avoid you as if you have leprosy. My situation may even remind them of their own personal experience of cancer or of someone who had cancer and they do not want to bring to surface from the depths of inner parts of their mind the pain that they have gone through. This is where my other chameleon color comes in.

When alone my mind is in turmoil; it is constantly making my daily life one of contrasts, like a yo-yo that is ever moving up and down. One moment I may be up and the next I may be at the bottom of the yo-yo's cycle; a cycle that is in perpetual motion denying the laws of physics. I am in a 24/7 mode of operation as there appears no escape from the reality of cancer. It is there with you when you wake up, it is there with you in the morning hours, it is there with you when you go to the store, it is there with you when you may be entertaining, it is there with you when you're watching television at night, it is there with you when you go to bed and you pray to God for healing, it is there when for some reason you wake up during the night; it is always present, never ending. How do you explain that to someone who has not walked in the same shoes and does not have a grasp of the terrible experiences that cancer brings? In some ways, I think the mental aspects of dealing with cancer may be as bad or worse then the physical aspects of dealing with cancer.

I wish I had a magic formula to give you as you go through many trials, but I do not. Well-intended people may say "just rely upon God", "out of adversity there comes good", "I know you will be ok", or "there are a lot of new treatments today that will help you". Well, thanks, but this does not help. Sure, I appreciate their sincerity and attempts at giving hope, but words alone do not provide peace of mind; words do not heal.

I may sound cynical and maybe I am to some extent. However, as I have tried to come to grips with cancer, I know I could not continue without drawing upon the strength given to us through our belief in God and the many comforting verses found in His Word. Does it totally solve my daily mental gyrations; no, but I cannot imagine what it would be like without His love and care for me to minimize those gyrations. I wonder how do those with cancer who do not have a relationship with God ever make it through the day? Where is their hope? The answer is they have no hope! You see I believe God truly understands my *situation. And I fully understand that my way may not be His way.*

There are many great Bible verses that give comfort and strength. Some of my favorites are found in the book of Philippians, such as:

"Rejoice in the Lord always. I will say it again: Rejoice! Let your gentleness be evident to all. The Lord is near. Do not be anxious about anything, but in everything, by prayer and petition, with thanks-giving, present your requests to God. And the peace of God, which transcends all understanding, will guard your hearts and your minds in Christ Jesus. Finally, brothers, whatever is true, whatever is noble, whatever is right, whatever is pure, whatever is lovely, whatever is admirable-if anything is excellent or praiseworthy-think about such things. Whatever you have learned or received or heard from me, or seen in me-put it into practice. And the God of peace will be with you." Philippians 4:4-9 (NIV).

And:

"Forgetting what is behind and straining toward what is ahead, I press on toward the goal to win the prize for which God has called me heavenward in Christ Jesus." Philippians 3:13b-14 (NIV).

Finally, I return to the scripture quoted at the beginning of this writing, Psalm 91 (NIV): A Psalm of hope and comfort. How can we not find solace when we read the following about God?

- *we will rest in the shadow of the Almighty*
- *He is my refuge and my fortress, … in whom I trust*
- *He will save you*
- *He will cover you with his feathers*
- *under His wings you will find refuge*
- *His faithfulness will be your shield and rampart*
- *He will command his angels to guard you in all your ways*
- *He will protect you, when we acknowledge His name.*
- *He will be with you in trouble*
- *He will deliver you and honor you*

Do I expect my life to be a "bed of roses" because I put my trust in His words of hope and comfort? No. Do I expect that this life will pass away and there will be a more glorious life for eternity with our Lord and Savior? Yes.

May you seek comfort in knowing that what is coming is far greater than what you are going through now.

Bruce W. VanderKolk (5 November 2017)

November 10, 2017 (Bruce)

It's a very slippery slope. Saw the doctor this morning and the doctor is sending me back to the cancer facility to see what they recommend next. Maybe they have some other treatments that might be more effective as the treatments I have taken are not totally getting rid of the cancer. The doctor did say it is better than when we started, but should be making more progress.

The doctor also stated that in rare instances the cancer can spread even though it has not gone through the bladder wall. Not very encouraging. Maybe two steps forward and one step back but never on firm footing.

December 13, 2017

Met with a doctor at the cancer facility this morning. Does not appear to be any alternative treatments that this doctor would recommend. There are two potential alternatives, these are:

1. *A clinical trial titled "A Phase III, Open Label Study to Evaluate the Safety and Efficacy of Instiladrin (rAd-IFN/Syn3) Administered Intravesically to Patients with High Grade, BCG Unresponsive Non-Muscle Invasive Bladder Cancer (NMIBC) Protocol no: rAd-IFN-CS-003). It has a potential of 30% cure over one year.*
2. *Removal of the bladder. This is really the only sure way of removing the cancer, however, it is a major surgery of about 6 hours and has a lot of potential risks, similar to open heart surgery.*

Trying to decide which is the best way to go. I have reservations about the clinical trial as side effects can be several, and similar to the treatment. Waiting to hear from the doctor on some questions that I had.

December 19, 2017

A decision has been made. I called the doctor's office today and said I want to go with removing the bladder. They moved fast. Surgery set for January 11, 2018 at 7:15 am. January 3rd I have a day of meetings and pre-op testing plus a CT scan of my chest. Not sure why my chest as on Dec 20th I have a CT scan of the urology track. I am at peace with this decision, realizing it is a long surgery, several risks, and an altering life style in the future.

Trust AND Obey (Roger)

Everyone who has attended Sunday School class learned the song "Trust and Obey". It was actually also a hymn sung in many churches prior to the modern worship music movement as well. Growing up, we sang the song often in church, so Dad would have been very familiar with the song.

If you learned the song, right now you are singing it in your head. Such a simple song with lyrics that were easy to learn and remember. But the lyrics of the song are deeper theologically than we can ever fathom this side of heaven.

According to online searching, the actual, scriptural foundation of the song is unknown, but a good candidate is found in Proverbs 3:

"Trust in the Lord with all your heart and lean not on your own understanding; in all your ways submit to him, and he will make your paths straight." (Proverbs 3:5-6, NIV)

Trust:

What's interesting is that many, if not most, mainline translations of the Bible have settled on the word "trust" to start this passage. The New International Version (NIV), the King James Bible, the New King James Bible, the Amplified Bible, the New Living Translation, etc. They all agree that the English word "trust" is appropriate to the intent of this passage. But what does it mean to trust?

Trust is one of those words that can be either a verb or a noun. Both are relevant to our understanding of the importance of trusting as recorded in the above Scripture. As a noun, the word "trust" speaks to the *act* of placing our reliance on someone else or to have hope for the future. As a verb, the word "trust" speaks to the *action* of placing our reliance upon someone else or to have hope in the future.

Which version of "trust" is important for us as we seek to emulate this passage? Both. In order to trust God we cannot simply say that we place our trust in Him. We need to actually do the verb and place our trust in Him.

Remember the activity in corporate picnics where there is a Trust Fall? The goal of the activity was to demonstrate that we could trust our co-workers to catch us when we fell backwards into their arms. This is the level of trust that we need to place in God as we go through our struggles: Eyes closed, falling backward into the unknown, and a complete loss of control in the outcome. This is how Dad lived his life during his struggles through prostate and bladder cancer: He trusted that God would catch him and deliver him safely.

Trust God. He will catch you.

Obey:

Proceeding on from the word "trust" in the above passage, the next phrases describe the act of obedience: "and lean not on your own understanding; in all your ways submit to him..". There are two key ideas with how we can obey: Get out of our head and acknowledge ALL of our plans before God.

First, we need to forget what our human nature tells us about living this thing we call life. Most of our ideas are junk to begin with, but the more we think of the path forward in our limited finite minds, the farther we are from God's plan and purpose for our time on this earth. All of us think we are the smartest people in the room. And in some instances, you may be the smartest man or woman in the room. But our intelligence pales in comparison to God and His wisdom.

How do we get out of our heads and "lean not on our understanding"? Spend time daily in the Bible. Pray. Spend time with wise people and seek their counsel. Don't over-think it because the probability is high that your thoughts (IE: "understanding") are going to be wrong anyway.

The second thing we need to do is to "submit ourselves to God". Other translations use words such as "acknowledge" and "recognize" in place of the word "submit". Once we have acknowledged that our way is not necessarily the best way forward, we need to look for guidance from God as to how to proceed. Once we have received that guidance, we actually need to act upon it and put it into practice in our daily lives.

Dad definitely understood this admonition: he continually searched scripture and prayed for God's guidance in his daily life. Dad would spend hours on the computer in the den searching for ways to submit himself to God. He would spend hours reading the Bible or self-help books in his recliner. When God directed him towards certain paths, he did his best to follow that direction.

Trust **and** Obey

What happens when we Trust **and** Obey God? He promises to "make our paths straight". Other passages describe God's action as "directing our paths". Notice that the passage doesn't say that He will eliminate all of the struggles we are facing or that life will be easy for us. Nope. What He will do is to be with us during this life, preparing us for the next life.

Remember the "Footsteps" poem that became a popular item of our culture back in the 1970's? The power of the poem was that it created a visual metaphor of how God walks with us as we navigate through difficult circumstances in our lives. When we trust and obey God, He promises to carry us through.

Dad trusted that God would heal him of his diseases, either in this life or the next. But Dad also provided numerous instances where he obeyed God while trusting in Him. Dad continued to serve in various leadership capacities at his church in Florida, even as he was fighting bladder cancer. He continued ministering to those less fortunate than himself. He was actively involved in missions committees and supported efforts at improving lives not only in his Florida community but around the world as well. Dad obeyed by teaching classes at church when requested.

One of the most visible examples of Dad's obedience was his tireless efforts to expand the physical footprint of the building at the church he attended in Florida. Dad firmly believed that more people need to experience God and felt that the church building needed to be expanded in order to reach more people. Dad was a key member of various building committees and teams. Because of the trust and obedience of Dad and many others within the congregation, the expanded building now brings new people into the church building every week.

Dad provided a great example of how to obey even in the worst of circumstances. There were many days when he didn't even want to get up out of bed or out of his recliner. After a sleepless night of sleeping in the recliner, the last thing he wanted to do was to go outside the house and seek how to serve God. But he knew that God had other things in store for his day. Dad's example shows that we don't have to be in perfect physical or mental condition to serve God and improve the lives of others.

Have you placed your trust in God? If so, where or how is He calling you to obey?

Conclusion

Blissful Ignorance

Dad's journal is finished: his last entry was on 12/19/2017. For reasons unknown, he didn't record highlights from the Christmas and New Year's holidays. Nor did he make any journal entries in the few weeks in early January leading up to surgery.

On December 22, 2017, I flew to SWFL to spend the holidays with Dad and Mom. My brother had to work so unfortunately he and his family were unable to join us. On the 24th I met up with a close college friend and his family in Venice, FL. We rented a pontoon boat and enjoyed the sun, sand, water, and great friendships. I drove back to Dad and Mom's in the evening where we went to church and then drove through a local community that provides an over-the-top holiday light experience. It was a great day.

Christmas Day was filled with the usual gift exchange, a family meal, and then ended with card games with family and friends. It was a great and busy day. Two of my favorite photos at that time were taken the next day: Mom and Dad exhausted, snoozing in their recliners.

On the 29th we joined a group from Dad and Mom's church to watch a game of the Florida Gulf Coast University's women's basketball team. Dad, Mom, my aunt, and my uncle had taken a liking to the sport and enjoyed watching them play. They went to several games. On this particular evening, the FGCU women won the game versus a determined South Dakota State team. The highlight of the evening for me was sharing my family's passion and enthusiasm for the game and fellowshipping together. And the popcorn.

New Year's Eve brought on the traditional get together between the VanderKolk and Chitwood (minister) families. We met together at Dad and Mom's house to celebrate the potential of the upcoming year. The food was a catered offering of tacos from a local restaurant. We spent the evening with family and friends, eating too much, playing cards, socializing, and laughing a lot.

It was a great holiday season and a welcome end to a tumultuous year. We were all ready to move on to bigger and better things in 2018.

However, none of us had any suspicion that this would be our last holiday season with Dad.

Epilogue

Dad's journey shifted in early January, 2018 towards a heavy focus on the medical visits required to ensure a successful surgery to remove the bladder. These experiences are unique and will be told in a third book of the series.

Dad's tale will come to a conclusion as we see how he thrived during his last weeks and days. More importantly, we will share how he created a legacy of thriving. This is something that has endured beyond his passing to today and will continue into the future.

PART FOUR
AFTERWORD

Personal Note

This has been a difficult book to write. The process of going through dad's writings continued to open fresh wounds caused by losing a beloved family member unexpectedly and too soon. In many respects, writing this book was more emotionally taxing than writing the first book. I kept finding myself hoping for a successful conclusion to Dad's fight while I was writing.

Dad's passing left his family and close friends in a state of complete shock. We all felt that if there was anyone who could outlast cancer, it was Dad. Everyone believed that Bruce's mission on earth wasn't finished; he had a lot more of himself to give the church, his friends, acquaintances, and yes, his family. More than once, the question, "What would Bruce have done?" was asked at home or at a leadership level at the church. His loss left a huge void in the lives of many. Including mine.

When this book is published, it will have been five years since Dad went to his heavenly reward. Time, we have found, does nothing to remove the loss of him in our everyday lives. The pain isn't as raw, but there remains a void in our lives.

We are grateful that the first book resonated with people going through significant struggles in this life. It is our hope and prayer that this book continues that legacy and readers continue to experience hope after reading Dad's journals. We are absolutely certain that Dad's intent with the journals was to be a blessing to others. We can only hope that this book will help accomplish his dream.

Thank you for taking this journey with me.

I hope this book has been a blessing to you and that you celebrate Dad's legacy in an upcoming book.

Acknowledgments

First and foremost, I have to express my forever gratitude to my father, Bruce VanderKolk. Even after he passed, he continues to help me on my journey through this experience we call life. I was blessed beyond measure to be raised in a home where both parents were believers. They did everything in their power to ensure that their children were provided what was necessary to push them on their faith journey to become children of God.

The bulk of this book is taken from the journal Dad wrote during all of his battles with cancer and other serious illnesses. How he was able to sit at his computer and type these words are beyond my comprehension. He fought through physical ailments and mental anguish at reliving the situations as he wrote his journal.

The book itself is a result of a simple question by Mom (Donna): "Why not take Dad's journal and turn it into a book? Surely it could help people." This was late 2021, three and a half years after Dad had passed. Thanks Mom for everything: You gave us life, nurtured us, pointed us in the right direction to go in life. You made sure that we developed a relationship with God so that one day, we will see Dad again. You were absolutely correct: Dad would have wanted this journal to be made available to others.

I also would like to thank Jeff and Judy Chitwood, ministers to our family for over 30+ years. We owe such a debt of gratitude towards the guidance, ministry, love, support, encouragement, leadership, and friendship that both of you have shown to my family. We are blessed that God led us to the church in Springfield so many years ago. Jeff: your review of the verses included in the Guide to Thriving section and suggestion of more appropriate verses is greatly appreciated.

Thanks to those of you who reviewed early copies of the manuscript: Donna, James, Shelia, Mary Lou, Don, Sandy, and Betty. Your suggestions made this a better book.

Thanks to Donna Hutcherson for all your editing work to turn a collection of random thoughts and poor grammar into a work that will honor Dad. Thanks for your patience throughout the back-and-forth process as it takes a while for things to sink into this Dutchman's head. I am forever grateful for your involvement with these projects.

PART FIVE
GUIDE TO THRIVING

Guide to Thriving

By and large, Dad approached life from a military point of view: It is better to be prepared and not require the plan you made, than to need the plan and not be prepared. This mentality served him well as he fought through all of the serious illnesses mentioned in this book.

The purpose of printing his journal is to equip those going through similar struggles by pulling lessons from Dad's life. Although the keys are found throughout Dad's journal, this section of the book is meant to provide an opportunity to focus specifically on those lessons and consider their application. This guide is to serve as a regular resource as you walk through your valley and fight to Thrive in the midst of your struggle.

I encourage you to read and meditate / pray on each of the 21 lessons and to write encouragements to your future self so that you can continue to thrive amidst your journey.

1. Trust

<u>Key to Thriving:</u>

Trust is required when the road or path we are walking becomes obscured by forces beyond our control. We need to trust that our doctors are acting in our best interest when we are going through medical issues. We need to trust that our friends and family have our backs and are supporting us when we are going through struggles.

But above all, we need to place our trust in God that when we believe in Him and accept His love for us, our struggles are only temporary. There is a better life coming.

<u>Bruce's Legacy on Thriving:</u>

There are many examples throughout Dad's life when he showed us that the best way to live this life is by putting our trust in God. The obvious example of trust in his life was when he was a young lieutenant in Vietnam. He worked in the artillery corps and they were routinely bombed by the enemy. There were countless nights where he had two choices during the bombardment: Option one was to put his trust in God's protection and get a decent amount of sleep. Option two was to worry all night and go crazy due to lack of sleep. He chose option 1 and that decision became the foundation of his life.

Dad trusted God in Vietnam. He trusted God when he was fighting prostate cancer. And as we read in this book, he put his trust in God while fighting bladder cancer.

<u>Foundation in Scripture:</u>

"May the God of hope fill you with all joy and peace as you trust in him, so that you may overflow with hope by the power of the Holy Spirit." (Romans 15:13, NIV)

<u>My Notes / Action Plan:</u>

2. Hope

Key to Thriving:

Hope is the key. Hope is the belief that today is going to be better than yesterday and that tomorrow is going to be better than today. Hope is not rational but it is necessary for us everyday.

As we go through struggles during this life, hope is the force that gets us out of bed every morning. Hope is the power to go about our day, living to our full potential. Hope is what keeps us going in the face of setbacks during our journey.

For the non-believer, hope is based on things improving in this life. For the believer, our hope is based upon the promise of God that life will be restored to its original intent in the next life. We are not promised an easy earthly life, but rather hope is His assurance that we will be renewed and restored to Glory in the next life.

Bruce's Legacy on Thriving:

When Dad passed away, we found a (very) small degree of relief that his struggles with his earthly body were finished. Over the course of his life, Dad struggled with:

- Nerve condition which made his writing indecipherable
- Multiple types of skin cancer
- Severely broken foot that made proper alignment and long walking impossible
- Prostate cancer
- Diabetes
- Blindness in his dominant eye
- Thyroid issues
- Injuries received as a result of a bicycle accident
- Multiple hernia surgeries
- Shoulder surgery
- Bladder cancer

Despite all of these, or perhaps because of them, Dad clung to the hope of ridding himself of the earthly body in exchange for a new one in Heaven.

Foundation in Scripture:

"Let us hold unswervingly to the hope we profess, for he who promised is faithful." (Hebrews 10:23, NIV)

My Notes / Action Plan:

3. The Only Easy Day

<u>Key to Thriving:</u>

"Congratulations! You made it through another rough day! Great job! You're awesome!" These are words that we would do well to practice saying to ourselves, saying them often enough to the point that we actually believe them. Write them on paper and leave them as notes to yourself throughout the day in the car, at your workspace, on the bathroom mirror, and even on the outside of the refrigerator.

Our world is fallen. As believers, we have the promise that tomorrow truly will be better than today; tomorrow is defined as either the literal next day or the next life. During our struggles we join with all Creation in expectation of when all of our pains and trials will be erased tomorrow.

As we struggle through today, let us look forward to the potential of tomorrow. Let's approach tomorrow with a positive mindset, excited by the reality that we have made it through today.

<u>Bruce's Legacy on Thriving:</u>

The military has embraced the concept that the only easy day is yesterday, particularly the special operations community. There are numerous books, articles, blog posts, and even t-shirts with this saying.

This is perhaps fitting because whether he knew it or not, Dad lived this motto during the end of 2017 and the beginning of 2018. During the holiday time period, we were able to drive onto the home of the special operations headquarters in Tampa, FL. Using Dad's Brigadier General credentials, we were able to drive through the gate, although the guard did ask Dad whether he was there under his own power (HaHa!). We drove past the headquarters buildings, officer housing, the memorial to fallen soldiers, and even had pizza for lunch at a local restaurant.

Did Dad really want to be there? Probably not. He was likely in pain and resting in the hotel bed would have been more comfortable. But Dad realized that in order to maintain a positive mindset he needed to look forward to greater things today than his struggles yesterday. During that same trip we also went to the shooting range and sent some lead downrange together and went golfing with his brother-in-law and a friend from church. Memories from those couple of weeks will last a lifetime.

Are you excited by today's potential or still fighting yesterday?

Foundation in Scripture:

"We know that the whole creation has been groaning as in the pains of childbirth right up to the present time." (Romans 8:22, NIV)

My Notes / Action Plan:

4. Holidays

<u>Key to Thriving:</u>

Science tells us that human beings cannot constantly be in a state of stress and worry. When we are constantly in fighting mode during a health struggle, we actually increase the stress on our lives exponentially. Mentally and physically, in order to be effective in our struggles, we need a break sometimes.

God gave us the perfect example in the book of Genesis where it is recorded that He took a break from creation on the seventh day. This was referred to as the "Sabbath" and has been carried down through the generations as an important day of rest.

We would do well to recognize this example in our lives and take a break to focus either on our mental health or on those around us, or both, as we walk through our struggles.

The same is true for holiday seasons. As we go through difficult journeys, it is extremely tempting to focus on ourselves during the holiday season. But much like the day of rest during the typical week, we need time where we can spend multiple days with friends and families. The quality time we are able to spend with them will create laughter that will take your mind off the struggle. Memories will be made. Fellowship will strengthen you mentally and physically.

In order to thrive through our struggle, sometimes we have to take a couple of days off and the holiday season provides the perfect opportunity for a break.

<u>Bruce's Legacy on Thriving:</u>

When they lived in Northern Illinois, Dad and Mom realized that the holidays weren't meant just for family and friends. The holidays are times when we need to step outside of our close relationships and assist others. At a time when most people were sprawled out on the couch or recliner taking the traditional turkey nap or watching football, Dad and Mom were usually serving the meal at a local homeless shelter. They volunteered in the midst of all of Dad's struggles. Or perhaps, they wanted to volunteer to help others because it would take their minds off of Dad's health struggles.

What can you do to make the upcoming holidays special?

"By the seventh day God had finished the work he had been doing; so on the seventh day he rested from all his work. Then God blessed the seventh day and made it holy, because on it he rested from all the work of creating that he had done." (Genesis 2:2-3, NIV)

My Notes / Action Plan:

5. Leaning on Friends

<u>Key to Thriving:</u>

Friends are necessary for a multitude of reasons. They make us laugh when we don't feel happy. They support us when we make mistakes or get into trouble. They let us crash at their place when we come in from out of town for a visit rather than paying for a hotel room. They let us borrow a cup of milk because ours has been in the refrigerator way past the expiration date. And they provide support for when we are going through hard times.

When I was writing this section, I happened to think of a friend who was going through a hard couple of years. So I phoned him. I didn't have any magic solution for his struggles, I just listened to him and supported him with ideas or comments. Likewise, he listened to me as I explained some of my issues and provided support for me during my walk.

Good friends like this friend are treasures and vital to our ability to thrive during difficult periods in our life.

<u>Bruce's Legacy on Thriving:</u>

Dad had many good friends in his life. He had friends that would discuss theological and church issues with him while at church or over lunch. He had friends that would listen to him and offer sage advice throughout his struggles. He had friends that would reach out to him via email, text, card, or the phone to see how he was doing while he was fighting the various types of cancer. He had friends that would create laughter while playing cards, golfing, or various other activities.

I can still remember one friend in particular that reached out to Dad over the phone quite often. Dad treasured these calls.

Dad realized that he needed friends to share his burden if he was going to make it through cancer. Dad wasn't usually an outgoing person, but throughout his cancer fight, he did make it a point to reach out to friends. He needed to lean on them for strength when he was struggling through a rough day. Dad also made it a point to reach out to friends that were going through their own struggles so that they could lean on him for strength.

Foundation in Scripture:

"Carry each other's burdens, and in this way you will fulfill the law of Christ." (Galatians 6:2, NIV)

"One who has unreliable friends soon comes to ruin, but there is a friend who sticks closer than a brother." (Proverbs 18:24, NIV)

"Therefore encourage one another and build each other up, just as in fact you are doing." (1 Thessalonians 5:11, NIV)

My Notes / Action Plan:

6. Manageable Goals

Key to Thriving:

The human brain is an amazing organ that is capable of so much more than we can ever grasp or understand. Unfortunately, because we are separated from God due to sin, we will never capitalize on this potential until we pass on to eternity in Heaven.

One of the drawbacks of this fallen condition is that when presented with a huge project or a task, our brains become overloaded and we get bogged down in brain fog. Or worse, we can become panicked when we don't see a way through to completion of the project.

Sound familiar? Are you facing a huge task right now that seemingly can't be accomplished? In order to assist your brain with creating a workable plan towards a solution, it may be necessary to break down the HUGE project into small items that are manageable. Make a list of these small projects and then cross them off when they are complete. This helps your mind recognize that you are making progress towards the end goal.

Bruce's Legacy on Thriving:

Dad was always working on projects, whether they were gardening, woodworking, home improvement, or projects for the family. For each project, he was diligent about making a detailed set of plans. These plans were important to Dad for a couple of reasons. First, the plans showed the path from project start to completion, outlining all of the smaller sub-projects, helping him to ensure that the final project would be acceptable when finished.

Secondly, the plans helped spur him on towards completion when the project was a long one. It was motivational to see the progress that he had already made.

Dad continued working on projects even when he was fighting bladder cancer. One of most relevant of these was that he continued working on the set of binders he created that detailed to his family the plans and information necessary in case of his early passing. These binders were extremely useful in the days immediately after his passing. This was a large undertaking, but Dad accomplished it one step at a time.

<u>Foundation in Scripture:</u>

"Noah did everything just as God commanded him." (Genesis 6:22, NIV)

"By faith, Noah, when warned about things not yet seen, in holy fear built an ark to save his family. By his faith he condemned the world and became heir of the righteousness that is in keeping with faith." (Hebrews 11:7, NIV)

<u>My Notes / Action Plan:</u>

7. Secondary Mission

<u>Key to Thriving:</u>

The first mission for us when we are in the valley of the shadow is to survive the journey; hopefully in a position to thrive during the struggle.

But we need a side project. Something to get us out of bed in the morning. Something where people depend on us. We need a secondary mission, something that distracts us from focusing on all of the negative developments and news during our struggle.

Your secondary mission could be something as minor as volunteering at a local charity on a regular (and frequent) basis. It could be something as massive as leading the charge to build a bicycle path on that old abandoned railroad track that goes through the center of your town. Most likely it will be something between these two examples. The important thing is that the mission is something that you become engaged in mentally and physically that is completely separate from your struggle.

What can be your secondary mission?

<u>Bruce's Legacy on Thriving:</u>

Dad had many secondary missions throughout his struggles with cancer. His largest was creation of the memorial to those from the county in northern Illinois that paid the ultimate sacrifice in wars. He participated in the creation of the project, instituted several project fund-raisers such as challenge coins and brick pavers. He worked with companies to provide donations. And he organized a major fund-raiser that secured the necessary funds to build the memorial.

<u>Foundation in Scripture:</u>

(Note: The first recommendation isn't necessarily an upbeat passage, but it is spot on: We all are going to leave this earth eventually and need to ask ourselves what we want to leave behind) "Whatever your hand finds to do, do it with all your might, for in the realm of the dead, where you are going, there is neither working nor planning nor knowledge nor wisdom." (Ecclesiastes 9:10, NIV)

"Whatever you do, work at it with all your heart, as working for the Lord, not for human masters." (Colossians 3:23, NIV)

"So whether you eat or drink or whatever you do, do it all for the glory of God." (1 Corinthians 10:31, NIV)

"And whatever you do, whether in word or deed, do it all in the name of the Lord Jesus, giving thanks to God the Father through him." (Colossians 3:17, NIV)

My Notes / Action Plan:

8. Outward Mentality

Key to Thriving:

Just as having a secondary mission helps to distract from your daily struggles, so does focusing on improving the lives of others. But this outward mentality has the added benefit of assisting your fellow man/woman.

This is radical thinking because it goes against our culture. Society tells us that if we want to "make it" in this world, we can't focus on others. We have to crush everyone beneath our feet. There are about a hundred passages in the Bible as to why this is an approach that we should not embrace. One of our purposes here on earth is to improve it and make it better when we leave it than when we arrived. If we focus on helping others, we accomplish this purpose.

Bruce's Legacy on Thriving:

Besides the examples already provided in this book, Dad did something important at every church where he was a member: he made sure he was a part of the missions committees. If you're not familiar, most churches have these committees; their purpose is to ensure that the church's financial contributions to various missionary organizations are purposeful. Dad made it clear to these committees that improving the lives of other people was critical to the churches' mission to bring people into a relationship with God.

Dad set a high bar for these missionary groups because it was important for him to improve the lives of others while he was in the midst of his struggle with cancer.

Foundation in Scripture:

"Serve wholeheartedly, as if you were serving the Lord, not people, because you know that the Lord will reward each one for whatever good they do, whether they are slave or free." (Ephesians 6:7-8, NIV)

My Notes / Action Plan:

9. Saints Among Us

<u>Key to Thriving:</u>

Recently the major news outlets reported a story about a famous Hollywood actor and a substantial financial gift that he was reported to have made to a charity.

I am not sure if the story is true but the spirit of the gift in this story is one that we need to emulate. We should give to others as a recognition of the bounties in life that have blessed us. When we give, we should give out of humility, not pride. As we look to embrace an outward mentality, there will be times when we cannot escape association with the gift. But there will be many times when we can give in secret so that the world does not give us praise for assisting the lives of others.

Most likely, the majority of us are not in a position to donate thousands of dollars to improve the lives of others. But we can do small things; actually, we must do small things. Remember the part of the book where Dad and Mom were blessed by members of the churches in Alabama when they evacuated from Hurricane Irma? Those people from that small town didn't get any recognition for donating a meal or a small gas card. But they certainly improved the lives of those people from Florida!

What is something small today that you can do, anonymously, that will improve the lives of others?

<u>Bruce's Legacy on Thriving:</u>

Dad's journal provided a few examples of where he and Mom helped someone in need of assistance. Not noted in the journal were many other instances of their generosity. They would regularly make a financial contribution to the church's emergency fund in order to provide food, shelter, or other assistance to those in need. They would sometimes pay for other's order in the drive-thru of fast food restaurants. There were countless others, all of which went unheralded and unrecognized.

Foundation in Scripture:

"So when you give to the needy, do not announce it with trumpets, as the hypocrites do in the synagogues and on the streets, to be honored by others. Truly I tell you, they have received their reward in full. But when you give to the needy, do not let your left hand know what your right hand is doing, so that your giving may be in secret. Then your Father, who sees what is done in secret, will reward you." (Matthew 6:2-4, NIV)

"Then he will say to those on his left, 'Depart from me, you who are cursed, into the eternal fire prepared for the devil and his angels. For I was hungry and you gave me nothing to eat, I was thirsty and you gave me nothing to drink, I was a stranger and you did not invite me in, I needed clothes and you did not clothe me, I was sick and in prison and you did not look after me.' 'They also will answer, 'Lord, when did we see you hungry or thirsty or a stranger or needing clothes or sick or in prison, and did not help you?' 'He will reply, 'Truly I tell you, whatever you did not do for one of the least of these, you did not do for me.' 'Then they will go away to eternal punishment, but the righteous to eternal life.'" (Matthew 25:41-46, NIV)

My Notes / Action Plan:

10. Worry Reduction

Key to Thriving:

This is one of the most difficult keys to thriving. How do you tell someone fighting a life or death illness not to worry? The answer, of course, is that you don't. From a human perspective, their worries are legitimate: Will I beat this disease? What will happen to my family? How will we financially recover from this? There are many potential reasons to worry.

But we cannot let worry deprive us of actually living. One of the best descriptions of the consequences of worry is found in a Scripture passage: "The seed falling among the thorns refers to someone who hears the word, but the worries of this life and the deceitfulness of wealth choke the word, making it unfruitful." (Matthew 13:22, NIV).

Although the passage specifically relates to those needing to come to God, that is a powerful picture of what worry does to us. Worry chokes us, making it difficult, if not impossible, to live, much less find enjoyment and fulfillment in this life.

Don't let worry grow to the point where it is literally choking the life out of you.

Bruce's Legacy on Thriving:

There were many things that Dad worried about during his struggles. One of the most prevalent worries had to be what would he do if he lost vision in his left eye and became totally blind? What would life be like?

We went to a shooting range on January 4, 2018. The possibility of losing his sight must have been on his mind because he had to adjust his shooting stance to only use his left eye. All his life he had practiced with his right eye and had become quite accurate. But now that he was unable to use his right eye, he had to worry about the future. But he put the worry behind him and concentrated on learning how to shoot with his non-dominant eye. As a result, we had a great day. Photos of him at the shooting range showed him relaxed and enjoying himself.

That was the last time we would go shooting together. I am thankful that he chose to not focus on his worry and instead lived his life that day.

Foundation in Scripture:

"Therefore I tell you, do not worry about your life, what you will eat or drink; or about your body, what you will wear. Is not life more than food, and the body more than clothes? Look at the birds of the air; they do not sow or reap or store away in barns, and yet your heavenly Father feeds them. Are you not much more valuable than they? Can any one of you by worrying add a single hour to your life?" (Matthew 6:25-27, NIV)

My Notes / Action Plan:

11. Pray

<u>Key to Thriving:</u>

Prayer is important as we go about our daily lives. But prayer is absolutely critical when we are struggling through difficult times such as fighting an illness or disease. The section in the text on prayer offered a Biblically-based example of HOW to pray.

Also important is the time WHEN we should pray. The answer should not surprise you: There is no bad time when to pray. Pray when you wake up in the morning. Pray when you are in the shower getting ready to start your day. Pray when you're in transport on your way to work. Pray during your lunch hour. As you might imagine, this also is relevant to WHERE to pray.

Prayer doesn't have to be long; it could just be a couple of minutes sometimes. Just follow the "ACTS" guideline.

The next item to consider is the WHO. Personally I have a difficult time praying non-stop for myself; it just seems disingenuous because I have many of my friends and acquaintances who are fighting harder battles than my own. I tend to focus on praying for them first. Only after I am satisfied with the amount of prayer for others do I pray for myself.

Find your own groove. But begin a concentrated prayer habit today.

<u>Bruce's Legacy on Thriving:</u>

Dad was no stranger to praying. As described in his journal, he prayed often, in many different circumstances. Most of his prayers were internal, simple conversations between him and God. But he and Mom were also advocates of praying before meals, whether the meal was at their house or outside the house in a restaurant. They went out to eat often and more times than not would join hands and pray for the meal, the server, and any friends or family that were with them during the meal.

Foundation in Scripture:

"And when you pray, do not be like the hypocrites, for they love to pray standing in the synagogues and on the street corners to be seen by others. Truly I tell you, they have received their reward in full. But when you pray, go into your room, close the door and pray to your Father, who is unseen. Then your Father, who sees what is done in secret, will reward you. And when you pray, do not keep on babbling like pagans, for they think they will be heard because of their many words. Do not be like them, for your Father knows what you need before you ask him." (Matthew 6:5-14, NIV)

My Notes / Action Plan:

12. Encouragement

<u>Key to Thriving:</u>

No matter what you are going through in your life as you read this, there are many others in our world who are not as blessed as you. Reading this book? There are millions around the world who can't read. Drowning in debt? There are millions around the world who don't have the ability to eat three meals and sleep indoors. Facing an incurable disease? You've been blessed to be able to wake up today.

So reach out to others and offer encouragement. Chances are you don't know their story and can end up being a blessing to them on their journey. Step away from yourself and brighten someone else's day.

<u>Bruce's Legacy on Thriving:</u>

Dad was not the type to reach out to others over long distances. He would make the occasional phone call or send an occasional email to his brother or to friends that lived far away. But send a card to someone? This rarely happened.

However, he was happy to talk to people in person about their struggles and was quick to offer words of support. This was perhaps his preferred manner of offering encouragement to friends, family, and acquaintances. Person to person.

But boy, did he relish those times when he received a card from someone. Emails and phone calls too. These all spoke volumes to him about the level of care that others had for him. These examples buoyed his spirits tremendously when someone reached out to him and offered encouragement.

<u>Foundation in Scripture:</u>

"Therefore encourage one another and build each other up, just as in fact you are doing." (1 Thessalonians 5:11, NIV)

"Praise be to the God and Father of our Lord Jesus Christ, the Father of compassion and the God of all comfort, who comforts us in all our troubles, so that we can comfort those in any trouble with the comfort we ourselves receive from God." (2 Corinthians 1:3-4, NIV)

"What, then, shall we say in response to these things? If God is for us, who can be against us?" (Romans 8:31, NIV)

"Never again will they hunger; never again will they thirst. The sun will not beat down on them,' nor any scorching heat. For the Lamb at the center of the throne will be their shepherd; 'he will lead them to springs of living water.' 'And God will wipe away every tear from their eyes.'" (Revelation 7:16-17, NIV)

My Notes / Action Plan:

13. Gray Days

<u>Key to Thriving:</u>

Gray days are a fact of life in this fallen world, unfortunately. Whether you have one gray day a month or twenty, they are serious because they throw life out of whack.

For this section, the author is not a doctor, just a lay person but offers two sources of help to get through gray days. The first is the Bible and the second is a qualified professional in your town. Solicit the qualified professional for assistance but refer to the Bible for assurance and comfort. Specifically relevant to these times in our lives is Psalm 23:

"The Lord is my shepherd, I lack nothing. He makes me lie down in green pastures, he leads me beside quiet waters, he refreshes my soul. He guides me along the right paths for his name's sake. Even though I walk through the darkest valley, I will fear no evil, for you are with me; your rod and your staff, they comfort me. You prepare a table before me in the presence of my enemies. You anoint my head with oil; my cup overflows. Surely your goodness and love will follow me all the days of my life, and I will dwell in the house of the Lord forever." (Psalm 23:1-6, NIV)

<u>Bruce's Legacy on Thriving:</u>

Dad's legacy on thriving for this topic is simply that he was not immune to gray days. When he was in the midst of the gray days he spent extra time in the Bible, searching for God's promises that the gray days are only temporary.

<u>Foundation in Scripture:</u>

"The Lord himself goes before you and will be with you; he will never leave you nor forsake you. Do not be afraid; do not be discouraged." (Deuteronomy 31:8, NIV)

"I waited patiently for the Lord; he turned to me and heard my cry. He lifted me out of the slimy pit, out of the mud and mire; he set my feet on a rock and gave me a firm place to stand. He put a new song in my mouth, a hymn of praise to our God. Many will see and fear the

Lord and put their trust in him." (Psalm 40:1-3, NIV)

"Then Jesus went with his disciples to a place called Gethsemane, and he said to them, 'Sit here while I go over there and pray.' He took Peter and the two sons of Zebedee along with him, and he began to be sorrowful and troubled. Then he said to them, 'My soul is overwhelmed with sorrow to the point of death. Stay here and keep watch with me.' Going a little farther, he fell with his face to the ground and prayed, 'My Father, if it is possible, may this cup be taken from me. Yet not as I will, but as you will.'" (Matthew 26:36-39, NIV)

"Cast all your anxiety on him because he cares for you." (1 Peter 5:7, NIV)

My Notes / Action Plan:

14. Procrastinating

<u>Key to Thriving:</u>

Are you someone that wants to get everything done as soon as possible or are you the type of person that wants to focus on something else during the near term and finish the projects later? Technically neither personality type is better than the other because God made us unique. Whether you finish the project today, tomorrow, or next month, what matters is that you finished the project.

But perhaps that thinking needs to be evaluated when it comes to serious issues, especially when we are fighting for our health. It likely isn't a good idea to put off the doctor's visit until next month if you were up all night vomiting. Procrastinating in that aspect of life isn't a behavior that will serve you well.

There are other areas of our lives where procrastinating should be minimized. Have a relationship that needs healing? It is probably a good idea to make the call today rather than when you "get around to it". Your boss put you on a deadline and promised to fire you if you miss the deadline? It is probably not wise to procrastinate to see if the ultimatum is serious.

<u>Bruce's Legacy on Thriving:</u>

Dad said the phrase "Don't put off until tomorrow what you can do today" so often during his life that the phrase might as well have come from the Bible. This was particularly true while we were growing up: chores had to be done ASAP rather than waiting until later in the day, or heaven forbid, tomorrow.

This mindset served Dad well as he was fighting prostate cancer, bladder cancer, and all of the other diseases he fought. Cancer is a very serious disease and he was not guaranteed a tomorrow. He wanted to make sure that if (or when) that day came, that he had no regrets when he looked back at his journey.

What are you putting off until tomorrow that should be done today?

Foundation in Scripture:

"My son, if you have put up security for your neighbor, if you have shaken hands in pledge for a stranger, you have been trapped by what you said, ensnared by the words of your mouth. So do this, my son, to free yourself, since you have fallen into your neighbor's hands: Go—to the point of exhaustion and give your neighbor no rest! Allow no sleep to your eyes, no slumber to your eyelids. Free yourself, like a gazelle from the hand of the hunter, like a bird from the snare of the fowler. Go to the ant, you sluggard; consider its ways and be wise! It has no commander, no overseer or ruler, yet it stores its provisions in summer and gathers its food at harvest. How long will you lie there, you sluggard? When will you get up from your sleep? A little sleep, a little slumber, a little folding of the hands to rest— and poverty will come on you like a thief and scarcity like an armed man." (Proverbs 6:1-11, NIV)

My Notes / Action Plan:

15. Hedges

There is a contrast in the Bible between the book of Genesis and the book of Job regarding the relationship between God and mankind. Chapter three of Genesis tells us that Adam and Eve enjoyed an actual, in-person relationship with God after they were created. In fact, verse 8 even goes so far as to say that God was "walking around in the Garden looking for them" (Genesis 3:8, NIV). How glorious that must have been, to have a direct relationship with the Creator of the universe! Unfortunately, when man sinned, this relationship was fractured; man no longer had a direct relationship with God.

But all was not lost. God continued to love mankind and promised to protect those that loved and followed Him. Our finite minds cannot comprehend the workings of God's protection, but God has given us the picture of placing hedges to protect those who believe in Him. Job was one such man: "blameless and upright; he feared God and shunned evil" (Job 1:1, NIV). God placed hedges around Job and continues to places hedges around His children today.

The challenge is that we don't know where God has placed the hedge around us. And our finite, human nature desperately WANTS to know the answer because it will provide a glimpse of the answer to our question: When is enough, enough?

We may never know the answer to this question. But we do know that God is all powerful. If we pray for God to adjust our hedges or the hedges of those that we care about, He will hear our prayers.

Bruce's Legacy on Thriving:
Dad fought various cancers between the years of 2014-2018 but God placed a hedge of protection around him; cancer did not end Dad's life. Nor did cancer end Mom's life when she was diagnosed with breast cancer in the 1980's. Their fights against cancer were not easy but looking back it is clear to see that God placed a hedge between their life's breath and cancer.

Foundation in Scripture:

"One day the angels came to present themselves before the Lord, and Satan also came with them. The Lord said to Satan, 'Where have you come from?' Satan answered the Lord, 'From roaming throughout the earth, going back and forth on it.' Then the Lord said to Satan, 'Have you considered my servant Job? There is no one on earth like him; he is blameless and upright, a man who fears God and shuns evil.' 'Does Job fear God for nothing?' Satan replied. 'Have you not put a hedge around him and his household and everything he has? You have blessed the work of his hands, so that his flocks and herds are spread throughout the land. But now stretch out your hand and strike everything he has, and he will surely curse you to your face.' The Lord said to Satan, 'Very well, then, everything he has is in your power, but on the man himself do not lay a finger.'" (Job 1:6-12, NIV)

My Notes / Action Plan:

16. Distractions and Diversions

Key to Thriving:

We have to take a break from our struggles. It seems counter-intuitive to step away from the fight, but our human minds and bodies cannot function at peak performance if we do not take time to recharge.

Consider top athletes, particularly those that specialize in marathons, triathlons, and other endurance events. Do enough research and you will find that one thing they have in common (in addition to physical talent, willpower not to eat snacks, etc.) is that they like to take naps. Perhaps "like" is not a strong enough word; they "need" to take naps so that their bodies can heal from the stresses of their past event or training. The nap helps to ensure that their body does not negatively affect their performance in the next event.

You and I are much the same (except for not eating snacks). When we are in the fights for our lives, we need to provide times of rest and relaxation. These times don't have to be a two-week vacation on an island in the Mediterranean Sea; they could be something as simple as a long nap.

What can you do today to take a break?

Bruce's Legacy on Thriving:

Dad was no stranger to naps. There are countless photos of him taking a nap on his recliner with a newspaper over his head. We always used to give him a hard time because of his napping habit. But looking back, we probably shouldn't have because he was using that time to get his mind back into sharp focus for work, church meetings, etc.

He and Mom would also go on trips as a diversion and distraction from his battles. They would drive a couple of hours, exploring the countryside. They would go on overnight trips to new areas. They continued going on cruises to see more of the world. They recognized that as hard as Dad was fighting, he needed break time as well.

Foundation in Scripture:

"The apostles gathered around Jesus and reported to him all they had done and taught. Then, because so many people were coming and going that they did not even have a chance to eat, he said to them, 'Come with me by yourselves to a quiet place and get some rest.' So they went away by themselves in a boat to a solitary place." (Mark 6:30-32, NIV).

My Notes / Action Plan:

17. Family

<u>Key to Thriving:</u>

There are three types of families: The family you are born into, the family you create, and the family you adopt. The family you are born into is pretty self-explanatory. Ironically, it is the one that is sometimes the most difficult in which to maintain healthy relationships. The family you create is your wife, husband, offspring, in-laws, etc. This family can also be somewhat of a challenge, especially in our culture of failed marriages. The final family, the one you "adopt", is all your close friends, those friends who are there for you when times are good or bad.

All three types of families are important to us as we struggle through this life because they provide love, comfort, support, and wisdom. Family is a source of strength, they are people that we can lean on while we are struggling.

Unresolved sin is usually the origin of rifts among family members. These rifts are important because they threaten the family's ability to provide a place for us to lean on during our struggles. They threaten our ability to thrive during our journey.

How is your relationship with your family? Is there a relationship that needs to be repaired?

<u>Bruce's Legacy on Thriving:</u>

Dad's goal was to repair and restore relationships among all his types of families as much as possible. In many of his relationships, he took the initiative to foster and strengthen the relationship. He made the calls or sent emails to family rather than waiting on a phone call from the other person.

When Dad passed on to the next life, there were very few relationships among his families that hadn't been repaired. He despaired over the relationships that were still fractured and regularly prayed for restoration to occur.

Foundation in Scripture:

"But if serving the Lord seems undesirable to you, then choose for yourselves this day whom you will serve, whether the gods your ancestors served beyond the Euphrates, or the gods of the Amorites, in whose land you are living. But as for me and my household, we will serve the Lord." (Joshua 24:15, NIV)

"Children, obey your parents in the Lord, for this is right. Honor your father and mother—which is the first commandment with a promise— so that it may go well with you and that you may enjoy long life on the earth. Fathers, do not exasperate your children; instead, bring them up in the training and instruction of the Lord." (Ephesians 6:1-4, NIV)

My Notes / Action Plan:

18. Good Samaritans

<u>Key to Thriving:</u>

One of the marks of maturity is sharing. When we are born, all that we care about is ourselves. This explains why children get into fights when they don't want to share their toys with the other little boys and girls. When we learned to share, we started the journey to become productive members of society.

Generosity is a component of sharing. When we are generous, we recognize that there are others less well-off than ourselves. We recognize that we could help others by sharing from the blessings we have been provided.

Generosity is another key to thriving because it also takes the focus off ourselves. When we practice generosity, we focus on others. We look to see if there is something that we can do or provide to help ease their journey. Generosity lessens the focus on our disease and struggle. Additionally, giving of our time and/or resources helps our struggle. This happens through the release of good feelings when we help others improve their situation.

<u>Bruce's Legacy on Thriving:</u>

In case you haven't caught on yet, a major theme of this portion of Dad's journal was an outward focus rather than an inward focus. The generosity and hospitality shown to Dad and Mom during their evacuation from Hurricane Irma made a lasting impact on them both. It is reasonable to assume that the other evacuees had similar experiences.

It would be interesting to go back and investigate the impact of the churches' generosity on society. Was there a "pass-it-on" component where the evacuees passed on that generosity to others they met while traveling back home? Did the concept grab hold? Are the evacuees continuing to practice this type of generosity even today?

Dad's other writings provide evidence that he felt compelled to manifest the spirit of generosity when he encountered people that were struggling.

Where in your life can you adopt the mentality of the people of Florence, AL? Are there people in your life that are struggling right now? What can you do to be a Good Samaritan to those people?

Foundation in Scripture:

"'Which of these three do you think was a neighbor to the man who fell into the hands of robbers?' The expert in the law replied, 'The one who had mercy on him.' Jesus told him, 'Go and do likewise.'" (Luke 10:36-37, NIV)

My Notes / Action Plan:

19. Everyday Evangelism

Key to Thriving:

Focus on others, not on ourselves. That is going to be one of our strategies as we are walking through the "valley of the shadow of death":

"The Lord is my shepherd;
    I shall not want.
    He makes me to lie down in green pastures;
    He leads me beside the still waters.
    He restores my soul;
    He leads me in the paths of righteousness
    For His name's sake.
    Yea, though I walk through the valley of the shadow of death,
    I will fear no evil;
    For You are with me;
    Your rod and Your staff, they comfort me.
    You prepare a table before me in the presence of my enemies;
    You anoint my head with oil;
    My cup runs over.
    Surely goodness and mercy shall follow me
    All the days of my life;
    And I will dwell in the house of the Lord
    Forever." (Psalm 23:1-6, NKJV)

"I shall not want". "My cup runs over". These passages confirm what we have discussed throughout this book: We are blessed. When death is knocking on our door, there are times when we will be in the midst of the valley.

Your dice has already been cast. What can you do today to help someone else through a very simple act of Everyday Evangelism? Lift your eyes from this page and look around you. What can you do? Whose life can you touch today?

Bruce's Legacy on Thriving:

Dad was a recipient of Everyday Evangelism when the elder asked whether he could pray for Dad after the meeting. This simple act: A question, likely a physical touch during the prayer, and a prayer to our Heavenly Father, meant the world to Dad. This simple act reminded Dad that indeed, we are the church. When we step outside of the physical church building, we are often the only glimpse of God that nonbelievers will see. Dad constantly was looking for ways to make sure that people saw God and not himself.

Foundation in Scripture:

"You are the salt of the earth. But if the salt loses its saltiness, how can it be made salty again? It is no longer good for anything, except to be thrown out and trampled underfoot. You are the light of the world. A town built on a hill cannot be hidden. Neither do people light a lamp and put it under a bowl. Instead they put it on its stand, and it gives light to everyone in the house. In the same way, let your light shine before others, that they may see your good deeds and glorify your Father in heaven." (Matthew 5:13-16, NIV)

My Notes / Action Plan:

20. Positivity

<u>Key to Thriving:</u>

Have you done it? Did you make a list of all the blessings in your life while reading the section in this book after October 26, 2017? If not, why not take a minute and start that list in the space provided below.

Everyday we wake up and make a choice: Do we want to grumble and hate the world today? Or do we want to approach the day with the gratitude for all that God has blessed us? Do we wake up with excitement at the potential that is to come today?

The Bible tells us to approach the day with positivity. Science tells us to approach the day with positivity. This book suggests that you approach the day with positivity.

Adopting a positive attitude in the middle of our struggles contributes to our emotional wellbeing and also becomes an example to others going through similar struggles. As previously mentioned, if you were speaking to my neighbor, he would be sure to remind you of the benefits of waking up with a positive attitude every day.

So what's stopping you? Be the light to someone else by being positive today.

<u>Bruce's Legacy on Thriving:</u>

Dad would be the first to tell you that he was not gifted with a positive personality. He was not one of those people who are such a joy to be around because they are always positive and upbeat. That wasn't Dad. About the only time when he employed the spirit of positivity was when we were on the golf course getting ready to tee off in front of water. "Think positive", we would encourage each other. He would respond, "I am. I am positive that I'm going to hit it into the water." Perhaps it is no surprise then that quite often the ball did in fact end up in the water.

But the lack of that gift didn't stop Dad from trying to wake up every day with a positive mindset. Throughout his journal we have read that when asked about how he was feeling, he tried to respond as positively as possible. He worked to be as positive as possible around his family and close friends.

Not too many of us are gifted with positivity. But what's stopping us from trying to develop that character quality?

Foundation in Scripture:

"Fear not, for I am with you; Be not dismayed, for I am your God. I will strengthen you, Yes, I will help you, I will uphold you with My righteous right hand." (Isaiah 41:10, NIV)

"Let nothing be done through selfish ambition or conceit, but in lowliness of mind let each esteem others better than himself. Let each of you look out not only for his own interests, but also for the interests of others." (Philippians 2:3-4, NIV)

My Notes / Action Plan:

21. Trust AND Obey

Key to Thriving:
When we can't see the outcome, we need to trust in a higher power than ourselves. Because sin came into this world, we are unable to see the end of our struggle while we are in the middle of the struggle. The best option for us is to simply just take the next step… and then the next, trusting in the One who created us.

But as we trust in God, we cannot forget the second part of that phrase: we must also obey. When we trust that God has a plan and a purpose for us in our struggle, we must be open to obey Him because in so doing, He positions us in the exact place for His plan.

We must trust.

We must obey.

We must trust AND obey.

Bruce's Legacy on Thriving:
Starting in the year 2014, Dad began a journey through multiple diseases that had the power to extinguish his earthly existence. Through it all, he trusted that God had a plan for him. Through it all he strove to obey God in order to be used by God.

Dad found comfort in the Bible throughout his struggle. It is reasonable to believe that he spent much time focusing on how to increase his trust in God. There are nearly 190 instances of the word "trust" in the New International Version of the Bible. There is little doubt that Dad read them all at least once, if not more times. The verses below are just a snapshot of the promises from God when we trust Him.

How is your trust in God? Are you ready to trust AND obey?

Foundation in Scripture:
"Trust in the Lord with all your heart and lean not on your own understanding; in all your ways submit to him, and he will make your paths straight." (Proverbs 3:5-6, NIV)

"I will love You, O Lord, my strength. The Lord is my rock and my fortress and my deliverer; My God, my strength, in whom I will trust; My shield and the horn of my salvation, my stronghold. I will call upon the Lord, who is worthy to be praised; So shall I be saved from my enemies. The pangs of death surrounded me, And the floods of ungodliness made me afraid. The sorrows of Sheol surrounded me; The snares of death confronted me. In my distress I called upon the Lord, and cried out to my God; He heard my voice from His temple, and my cry came before Him, even to His ears." (Psalm 18:1-6, NIV)

"Oh, taste and see that the Lord is good; Blessed is the man who trusts in Him!" (Psalm 34:8, NIV)

My Notes / Action Plan:

Appendices

Appendix A: Obituary

Bruce W. VanderKolk 3/16/1945 - 2/18/2018 Bonita Springs, FL— Bruce W. VanderKolk, 72, of Bonita Springs, FL and formerly of Oregon, IL, died Sunday, February 18, 2018. He was born March 16, 1945, in Allegan, MI, the son of Wiley and Violet VanderKolk. He married Donna Sue Townsend in 1968.

Mr. VanderKolk graduated from Hopkins High School in 1963 and from Michigan State University in 1967. He received his Masters degree in 1977 from the University of Illinois at Chicago. While at Michigan State University he was a member of the ROTC program and upon graduation he was commissioned a Second Lieutenant. He served in the active Army from 1967-1969 and was a Vietnam veteran. Upon leaving the active Army in 1969, he remained in the Reserve Components and retired in 1994 from the Illinois National Guard as a Brigadier General. He received the Legion of Merit, Bronze Star, Meritorious Service Medal with two oak leaf clusters and Army Commendation Medal with one oak leaf cluster.

After leaving the active Army, he joined the Illinois State Police in 1969 and served in a variety of positions, retiring in 2001 as the Commander of the Forensic Sciences Command. He was an Emeritus member of the American Society of Crime Laboratory Directors and Midwestern Association of Forensic Scientists.

He was a member of Anchor Christian Church in Bonita Springs, FL where he and his wife lived. He was a prior member of Southside Christian Church in Springfield, IL. While living in Oregon, IL, he attended the Oregon Church of God. He was a member of Oregon VFW Post 8739 and Oregon American Legion Post 97.

Mr. VanderKolk is survived by his loving wife of 49 years, Donna Sue; his sons, Roger VanderKolk of Woodbury, MN, and James (Shelia) VanderKolk of Oregon, IL; and seven cherished grandchildren, Ethan, Corey, Sean, Matthew, Nadia, Caelyn and Madilyn.

A funeral service will be held Thursday, February 22, 2018, at 11:00 a.m. at Anchor Christian Church, Bonita Springs. Visitation for family and friends will take place at the church from 10:00 a.m. until the time of the service. A celebration of life service will be held Thursday, March 1, 2018, at 5:00 p.m. at the South Side Christian Church, 2600 S MacArthur Blvd., Springfield, IL. Graveside services with Military Honors will take place Saturday, March 3, 2018, at 1:00 p.m. at Maplewood Cemetery in Hopkins, MI. In lieu of flowers, the family suggests that memorial contributions be made to the Anchor Christian Church Building Fund, 11651 E Terry Street, Bonita Springs, FL 34135.

Appendix B: Bruce Wiley VanderKolk Curriculum Vitae

Education
- Michigan State University, B.S. Police Administration w/ emphasis in Forensic Science 1967
- University Illinois at Chicago, MS, Criminalistics, 1977
- Command and General Staff Course, Military 1982

Forensic Science/Management Experience
- October 1995 - June 2001: (Retired) Commander, IL State Police, Forensic Sciences Command
- January 1978 - October 1995: Bureau Chief, IL State Police, Bureau of Forensic Sciences
- October 1977 - December 1977: Assistant Bureau Chief, IL Dept. Law Enforcement, Springfield
- February 1973 - September 1977: Laboratory Director, IL Dept. Law Enforcement, Maywood
- September 1970 - January 1973: Laboratory Director, IL Dept. Law Enforcement, Rock Island
- October 1969 - August 1970: Drug Chemist, IL Dept. Law Enforcement, Joliet

Forensic Science/Management Assigned Responsibilities

Commander: Served as Commander of the Forensic Sciences Command, Illinois State Police, which consisted of eight regional forensic science laboratories and a Research and Development laboratory, consisting of a total staff of 468. Oversaw and coordinated the prompt, accurate and appropriate delivery of laboratory analyses and polygraph examinations involving 110,000 criminal cases in support of criminal justice agencies within Illinois. Additionally, the States DNA Convicted Sexual Assault data base was implemented within the Forensic Sciences Command.

NOTE: During the early 90s, an agreement was reached between the City of Chicago and the Governor of Illinois in which the Chicago Police Department Crime Laboratory Function would be transferred to the Illinois State Police. I was responsible for managing the merger which consisted of determining which Chicago Police Department employees would be transferred, hiring the management staff, establishing systems to ensure the prompt and accurate analysis of approximately an additional 55,000 cases, hiring approximately an additional 150 new forensic scientists and providing appropriate training, and implementing a laboratory management information system to track evidence, provide reports, statistical data and online capabilities with the Cook County States Attorneys Office. In July 1996 the transfer was completed and one year later the laboratory received national accreditation by the American Society of Crime Laboratory Directors-Laboratory Accreditation Board.

Bureau Chief: Served as Bureau Chief of the Bureau of Forensic Sciences, Illinois State Police, which consisted of seven regional forensic science laboratories and a Research and Development laboratory, consisting of a total staff of approximately 310. Oversaw and coordinated the prompt, accurate and appropriate delivery of laboratory analyses and polygraph examinations in support of criminal justice agencies within Illinois. During this period the nations first Training and Applications Laboratory was established to train new forensic scientists plus the nations first formalize Quality Assurance Program was implemented. These two areas were important in that a sound training program was established to ensure well-trained forensic scientists were placed in the laboratories and the Quality Assurance program monitored statewide the accuracy, timeliness and completeness of forensic analyses.

NOTE: In 1985, the State's Forensic Toxicology program operating under the control of the Department of Public Health was transferred to the Illinois State Police by direction of the Governor due to improper management and analytical practices. I managed the transfer and because of issues determined that none of the current employees would be accepted. The function was relocated from the Chicago area to Springfield and all new staff were hired, facilities obtained, and policies/protocols developed.

Assistant Bureau Chief: Responsible to the bureau chief for administering support functions for several forensic laboratories, including, but not limited to, budget preparation, administrative transactions, policy/procedural development, training and quality assurance issues.

Laboratory Director - Maywood: Served as the laboratory director for the Maywood Forensic Science Laboratory. Responsible for providing forensic science services to the greater metropolitan Chicago area, excluding the City of Chicago. Directed the activities of several forensic science disciplines and administrative functions.

Laboratory Director - Rock Island: Served as the laboratory director for the Rock Island Forensic Science Laboratory. Responsible for providing forensic science services to the northwestern portion of Illinois. Directed the activities of forensic science disciplines, polygraph and crime scene investigation.

Crime Laboratory Analyst: Conducted forensic examinations in the areas of drug chemistry, arson and blood alcohol. Responsible for the interpretation and reporting of results of analyses to user agencies and subsequent court testimony.

Teaching: 1971 to 1972 - Instructor in forensic science/crime scene investigation at Blackhawk College.

Military Assignments

Numerous military assignments from 1967 to 1994, to include active duty in Vietnam; retired August 28, 1994, as Brigadier General, Illinois Army National Guard. During 27 years of military service, 15 years were involved as a commander of different units. These included company, battalion and brigade levels, plus command of the Illinois Military Academy. Also served as principle staff officer at battalion and brigade levels.

Professional Occupation Since Retiring From The Illinois State Police

April 2010 to December 2010

Served as the Executive Administrator for South Side Christian Church, Springfield, Illinois. After the Senior Minister left his position,

I was asked to oversee the ministerial and support staff of the church. Responsible for coordinating the staff at two campuses and overseeing the day to day operations of the church. Served as the liaison between the staff and the Board of Elders.

August 30, 2004 to December 31, 2006

Served as the Assimilating/Equipping Ministry Director for South Side Christian Church, Springfield, Illinois

Responsible for developing processes to involve church attendees in serving as a volunteer in one of the many volunteer positions; training leaders of volunteers to help improve their skills in recruiting, retaining and proper placement of volunteers; one of five members serving on the Vision Planning Team developing and overseeing the strategy planning process for the church.

August 1, 2001 to August 29, 2004

Served as the Church Administrator for South Side Christian Church, Springfield, Illinois. I was hired as the first church administrator and given responsibilities for supervising all of the support staff, managing the facilities, establishing policies and procedures, overseeing the budget and preparation of new fiscal year budgets (approximately 1.2 m), recruiting and assigning volunteers, and working on special projects either for the Senior Minister or Board of Elders.

Professional Organizations

- American Society of Crime Laboratory Directors (Served on legislative/strategic planning committee and Board of Directors), Emeritus Member
- Midwestern Association of Forensic Sciences, Charter Member, President, Secretary, Treasurer, Newsletter Editor, Emeritus Member
- Illinois Association of Identification
- National Guard Association of Illinois
- National Guard Association of United States
- Reserve Officers Association
- American Legion Post 97, Oregon, IL

- VFW Post 8739, Oregon, IL, Life Member

Professional Activities
- Assisted as a consultant to Bianchi Consulting, Ltd., reviewing selected areas of the New York Police Department Forensic Laboratory, March 2008.
- Served in various leadership training capacities to the following: Maritime Christian College in Prince Edward Island, Restoration House in New Hampshire, Anchor Christian Church in Bonita Springs Florida.
- Served on the Advisory Board to The Independent Investigator for the Houston Police Department Crime Laboratory and Property Room, April 2005 to June 2007.
- Trainer and Instructor for the Illinois Regional Institute for Community Policing on DNA: Evidence Identification, Collection, & Preservation for Law Enforcement, 2005, 2006
- Served as Lead Auditor & Human Resources Auditor, City of Phoenix, City Auditor Department, performing a Police Crime Laboratory Audit of the Phoenix Police Department, 2003-2004.
- On an informal basis prepared a Proposal for Forensic Services for Chief Terrance Gainer, Metropolitan Police Department, District of Columbia
- Served on a team in the late 1990s as a consultant to the New York Police Department Crime Laboratory to help prepare the laboratory for national accreditation by the ASCLD-LAB.
- Member, National Center for Forensic Sciences Advisory Board, University of Central Florida, 1997 to 2001.
- Trained as an Inspector for the American Society of Crime Laboratory Directors/Laboratory Accreditation Board (ASCLD-LAB), 1998
- Member of Forensic Science Evaluation Team to Ministry of Internal Affairs of Russia, 1997
- Delegate to 1994 International Forensic Science Symposium, Taiwan
- People to People Forensic Science Project delegate to the USSR,

1988.
- Served as a management consultant for Marion County Crime Laboratory, Indianapolis, Indiana performing an audit of the laboratory.
- Served on various ASCLD, MAFS, AAFS committees.

Professional Publication/Presentations:

Kreiser, M.J., Vander Kolk, B.W., "Leasing Analytical Instruments: Advantages, Disadvantages, and Contract Procedures," Journal of Forensic Sciences, 27 (3), July 1982, pages 598 - 621.

Several presentations at regional and national forensic science organizations.

Professional Awards:
- Midwestern Association of Forensic Scientists Distinguished Service Award, 1988
- American Society of Crime Laboratory Directors - The Briggs J. White Award, 1998
- Numerous military awards to include Legion of Merit, Bronze Star and Meritorious Service Medal with two Oak Leaf Clusters.
- Illinois State Police awards to include Meritorious Service Medal and Achievement Awards

Personal

Date of Birth: March 16, 1945, Allegan, Michigan
Marital Status: married, two children
Hobbies: cycling, walking, reading

References: Available upon request

(Updated April 30, 2015)

Bibliography / Notes / Resources

General Bibliography / Notes / Resources:
- Unless otherwise noted, all Scripture quotations are from THE HOLY BIBLE, NEW INTERNATIONAL VERSION®, NIV® Copyright © 1973, 1978, 1984, 2011 by Biblica, Inc.® Used by permission. All rights reserved worldwide.
- Bruce's writings are assumed to be attributed solely to his creation except in circumstances where he provides annotation for the author of the work.

"Who was Bruce VanderKolk?" Bibliography / Notes / Resources:
- This section could take many pages to list all of the accomplishments that Bruce gathered while on the earth. But doing so probably would have embarrassed him so this section has been left intentionally vague. Besides, while important to his family and friends, it would be less than meaningful to the average reader. If you are interested in learning more about Bruce and his accomplishments, there is always the option to perform an Internet search.
- The link between Agent Orange and adverse health affects on those serving in Vietnam is well established and common knowledge. As of the writing of this book, the U.S. Department of Veteran's Affairs has a dedicated web page specifically devoted to Agent Orange (https://www.va.gov/disability/eligibility/hazardous-materials-exposure/agent-orange/).
- What is not common knowledge is that Bruce was deemed eligible for disability consideration by the VA as a result of his exposure of Agent Orange while in Vietnam. As a family we believe that Bruce would have approved the release of this information to the general public.
- The "Personal Testimony" section was written by Bruce, with the calling out from the specific version of the Bible referenced in

190

the document. It was written in the midst of his fight with bladder cancer and was also included in the previous book about his battle with prostate cancer because the message is relevant all the challenges he experienced in his life. There is no doubt whether this was written by Bruce for himself or that it was written for others. Bruce wrote it to provide strength and encouragement to others going through similar battles and struggles.

"How then to Thrive?" Bibliography / Notes / Resources:
- This section is written entirely by the author.
- Bruce didn't use the word "thrive" in his journal nor in his writing. The intent of this section is to bring definition to Bruce's thought process when he was documenting his struggles. What did he want to accomplish? Was it for him? It clearly was for others. But why? What was the driving factor for this intensely private man to share his struggles with others? It is easy to determine that he wanted to help others as they navigated through life's struggles. As a family, we spent quite a bit of time discussing and feel that he wanted to help them thrive.
- The definitions of words are pulled from Webster's online dictionary (www.merriam-webster.com) at the time of the writing of the first book (est 2022).

Conclusion to Bruce's Story: 2014 Bibliography / Notes / Resources:
- Unless otherwise noted, all Scripture quotations are from THE HOLY BIBLE, NEW INTERNATIONAL VERSION®, NIV® Copyright © 1973, 1978, 1984, 2011 by Biblica, Inc.® Used by permission. All rights reserved worldwide.
- A few other translations of the word "overflow" are as follows: "Abound" (King James, New American Standard versions), "Abound and be overflowing (bubbling over)" (Amplified version).
- October 24, 2014: There are a lot of discussions about the urination process in this book. Writing these journal entries must have been difficult for Dad because he wasn't the sharing type. Having strangers know about his waste elimination tract would not have set well with him. This is

one of the reasons why we are sure he wanted this journal to be published: his discomfort was minor when compared to the potential to help others.

- Hope: There are many songs of hope in the Christian music scene that the reader can investigate. The lyrics of the suggested songs on this list couldn't be printed in this book due to copyright reasons but the reader is encouraged to start with these songs. These songs are strong reminders of the hope we have in God and Jesus. The reader is encouraged to search for these songs, listen, and to pay attention to the lyrics.

- November 10, 2014: Dad's original journal included much detailed information which appears that he copied directly from websites. This content in this section has been pulled from multiple sources, included commonly known information.

- PSA: The information about bladder cancer was pulled from the American Cancer Society's website on February 19, 2023. The author found this website to be very informative.

Conclusion to Bruce's Story: 2015 Bibliography / Notes / Resources:

- Unless otherwise noted, all Scripture quotations are from THE HOLY BIBLE, NEW INTERNATIONAL VERSION®, NIV® Copyright © 1973, 1978, 1984, 2011 by Biblica, Inc.® Used by permission. All rights reserved worldwide.

- January 16, 2015: Dad read the book "You'll Get Through This" written by Max Lucado. He was always a fan of Max Lucado. If you're not familiar, Mr. Lucado has been gifted with the ability to portray the written word into text that is easily digestible by the general public. Whether the topic is a passage from the Bible, an event from the Bible, or a challenging theological concept, Mr. Lucado brings words to life. Dad appreciated this style of writing and purchased many of Mr. Lucado's books and would read them often throughout his life.

- January 21, 2015: Dad also read the book "If God is Good" by Randy Alcorn and found it very relevant to his struggle with multiple, potentially life-altering diseases. Although Dad was a strong Christian who had followed God for the majority of his life, he questioned his lot in life while fighting cancer. This book played a significant role in Dad's belief that God was *with* him *during* the struggle.

- "Secondary Mission": The new VFW memorial that Dad helped bring to reality is a fitting tribute to those from northern Illinois that made the ultimate sacrifice for our country. If you ever find yourself in the town of Oregon, IL, take a few minutes to visit the memorial.

- July 8, 2015: The statistics and information that Dad included in his journal were as of his Last Medical Review on 02/26/2014 and was Last Revised by Dad on 02/25/2015. Detailed (and current) presentation of the survival rates of bladder cancer can be found at the American Cancer Society's website: https://www.cancer.org/cancer/bladder-cancer.html

- "Outward Mentality": Although the information that Dad gleaned from all of his online searches have been scrubbed from this book, the importance of this entry is the encouragement to conduct your own research when facing a difficult journey.

- "Saints" - Passage of scripture is from the NIV translation of the Bible of Matthew 25:31-46.

Conclusion to Bruce's Story: 2016 Bibliography / Notes / Resources:

- Unless otherwise noted, all Scripture quotations are from THE HOLY BIBLE, NEW INTERNATIONAL VERSION®, NIV® Copyright © 1973, 1978, 1984, 2011 by Biblica, Inc.® Used by permission. All rights reserved worldwide.

- March 9, 2016: The video series by Craig Groeschel that Dad wrote about in this entry is highly recommended for everyone, not just believers, as they go through serious struggles.

- Why Worry: The Bible verse in this section (Hebrews 11:1) is quoted from the King James Version.

- August 25, 2016: The quotations from the Guideposts Magazine articles were included in Dad's journal. Due to copyright reasons, I made the decision to pull these articles from this book. The reader is encouraged to go online and find the original articles because they offered a tremendous amount of encouragement to Dad.

- August 25, 2016: Dad really enjoyed receiving cards and well wishes from his friends and family; they made it seem like Dad wasn't going through his struggle alone. Some of the text on the cards that he recorded have been eliminated due to copyright reasons but the Bible verses were the important aspect on the card. Prior to reading Dad's journal, this was something that I hadn't really considered, writing a Bible verse on a Get Well card. **The family would once again like to thank all those who sent cards to Dad during his medical fights.**

Conclusion to Bruce's Story: 2017 Bibliography / Notes / Resources:
- Unless otherwise noted, all Scripture quotations are from THE HOLY BIBLE, NEW INTERNATIONAL VERSION®, NIV® Copyright © 1973, 1978, 1984, 2011 by Biblica, Inc.® Used by permission. All rights reserved worldwide.
- February 15, 2017: Faced with yet another potentially devastating disease, Dad went back to his habit of scouring online for information. He seems to have abandoned his practice of copying information directly from websites as the content in this section seems to have been summarized.
- March 1, 2017: More information summarized.
- October 26, 2017: Dad found a lot of comfort in the book "To Heaven and Back", written by Mary C. Neal, MD. His journal entry on October 26, 2017 focused on pages 100-101. As per his usual, Dad actually included the direct quote from the book in his journal. The reader is encouraged to purchase the book to read the words directly from Dr. Neal in this section.
- "Importance of a Positive Attitude": One of the blessings in my life is the community where I was able to purchase a house when I moved to Florida. Not only am I less than a mile from my mother's house, I am blessed to live across the street from the positive neighbor. He grew up in a working class background and blossomed into a powerful figure in women's collegiate basketball. When he retired from a D1 university, he was inducted into the state hall of fame for all his efforts. Thank you Tony!
- "Importance of a Positive Attitude": Readers from the first

book should remember the admonition to research the songs and lyrics found in the songs from Crowder's album, "Milk and Honey". The song mentioned in this section is from the album "I Know a Ghost". The reader is encouraged to review all the songs on this album as well. Actually, if your time schedule permits it, research all of Crowder's music. It will bring you closer to God.

- November 4, 2017: In his journal, Dad went into great detail to describe the procedure that the doctor performed to remove the cancerous spots in his bladder. But in his journal he directly copied the specific details from various websites so these have been eliminated to protect the copyright of the original author. If you are dealing with bladder cancer, more information can be found by typing the specific procedure that Dad recorded into a Internet search engine.

- December 13, 2017: Please remember that the two treatment alternatives presented to Dad were presented in the year 2017. Hopefully the medical community has discovered or created new treatment options since that time-frame. Please consult with your medical professional to determine the best options for your situation.

"Guide to Thriving" Bibliography / Notes / Resources:
- All Scripture quotations are from THE HOLY BIBLE, NEW INTERNATIONAL VERSION®, NIV® Copyright © 1973, 1978, 1984, 2011 by Biblica, Inc.® Used by permission. All rights reserved worldwide.

"Appendices" Bibliography / Notes / Resources:
- Bruce continued to update his "CV" (ie: Resume) even after he retired.

---

www.ingramcontent.com/pod-product-compliance
Lightning Source LLC
Chambersburg PA
CBHW051517120626
46551CB00012B/962